ISBN: 9781313776479

Published by:
HardPress Publishing
8345 NW 66TH ST #2561
MIAMI FL 33166-2626

Email: info@hardpress.net
Web: http://www.hardpress.net

THE
ART OF MIMICRY

By

J. ARTHUR BLEACKLEY

"Look at Nature and see how it affects your mind"
—Ruskin

NEW YORK
SAMUEL FRENCH
PUBLISHER
28-30, WEST 38TH STREET

LONDON
SAMUEL FRENCH, LTD
26, SOUTHAMPTON STREET
STRAND

Dedicated

To

MY MOTHER

CONTENTS

CONTENTS

CHAPTER I

Introduction

" **I** GAVE him an account of the excellent mimicry of a friend of mine in Scotland; observing at the same time, that some people thought it a very mean thing," said Boswell in his *Life of Dr. Johnson.* Dr. Johnson replied : "Why, sir, it is making a very mean use of man's powers. But to be a good mimick requires great powers ; great acuteness of observation, great retention of what is observed, and great pliancy of organs to represent what is observed." [1]

The art of mimicry, and the art of acting are almost identical ; only the mimic has gone a step further than the actor in exercising his powers of observation. He has more closely noticed the collateral species of the genus " type."

Acting is a mimicry of life ; as mimicry is a burlesque of the actor's art.

"Mimicry," said Mr. Max Beerbohm, in the *Saturday Review*, June 11, 1904, " is a thing that has always interested me. As is parody to literature,

---

[1] Boswell's *Life of Dr. Johnson.*

9

so (at its best) is mimicry to acting. The two things have this further point in common : each of them is for the most part a speciality of youth. Read any undergraduate journal, and you will find that it is mainly composed of parody, unconscious and conscious. Only a very precocious undergraduate has original thoughts and feelings. His soul is still vacant, gaping for the contents of other souls. It is still malleable, and may be from moment to moment moulded to any shape. Maturity fills it from within and fixes it, and thenceforth its owner has no power of parody, and no desire of parody. That is the normal course. But sometimes a mature man retains this desire, and this power. . . . Now the power of mimicry deserts the average man at the same time and for the same reason as the power of parody. Before he is twenty the average youth can catch more or less recognizably, the tone of voice, and the tone of mind of his friends. Later his own mind acquires so distinct a tone, and he becomes so accustomed to the sound of his own voice, that his efforts at mimicry (if he make any) are dire failures. Occasonally, however, a man retains the knack even in his prime, and even though he has a distinct individuality. In him, and in him alone, we behold the complete mimic. For mimicry is a form of criticism, and a distinct individuality—a point of view—is as needful in the mimic as in the critic. Mimicry that is a mechanical reproduction of voice and gesture, and facial play, is a mere waste of time and trial of patience. Yet that is the kind of mimicry that is nearly always offered to us. A man comes upon the platform and reproduces verbatim some scene of a recent play exactly as it was enacted by this or that mimic. If he were a parrot the effect would be amusing; for it is odd to hear a bird uttering human inflections. But he happens to be a man, and so we are merely bored. His method being an exactly faithful reproduction of his subjects, we have no inclination to laugh; and the only pleasure we might be expected to gain would be when the subject were one for which we had a profound admiration; but even so we should be more irritated than pleased. We should be wanting the real thing. An exact reproduction of the real thing can never be a satisfactory substitute, and if the average mimic is not a satisfactory subtitute, what in reason's name is he? The proper function of the mimic is, of course, like that of the parodist in words, or of the caricaturist in line, to exaggerate the salient points of his subject so that we can, whilst we laugh at a grotesque superficial effect, gain sharper insight into the subject's soul, or, more strictly, behold that soul as it appears to the performer himself." [1]

Alfred Miles urges his readers to avoid imitation in his *Standard Elocutionist*; he says: " Imitation may sometimes be the sincerest form of flattery, but

---

[1] Max Beerbohm: *A Play and a Mimic.*

it is quite as often the strongest proof of incapacity, if not of impudence and conceit, and it is a course which abounds in pitfalls for the unwary. Imitation is necessarily limited to the sphere of the physical, and the material. You may model the human eye in glass, but you cannot put the soul-fire into it. You may teach a parrot to quote Scripture, but you cannot put divinity into its utterances. You may yourself imitate the gesticulations of a master, but it will be mechanical as the movements of a working model without the master's spirit too. You may mimic the movements of form and limb, and the modulation of tone and voice, but not the vital force that makes the dead limb live, and fills the voice with inspiration. It is said that the young preachers of Robert Hall's time imitated him even to the pain in his back: and we have ourselves seen the young tenors of his generation imitate Mr. Sims Reeves even to his walk on the platform: but in all that made either models they were both inimitable. All that is mechanical in any art may be learnt from without, but that which is spiritual must be supplied from within. Thus the student who imitates gets the bodies of words and not the souls, the husk of thoughts but not the kernels, and on such fare he can but starve himself, and those who listen to him." [1]

This is perfectly true as a description of the false, counterfeit school of mimicry, which is to be avoided.

[1] A. H. Miles: *Standard Elocutionist.*

Mr. Max Beerbohm has very clearly pointed out the true, legitimate method of mimicry at its best.

You see there is a true and false school of mimicry. Let it be our business to cultivate the one and avoid the other.

Before studying the Art of Mimicry it is necessary to study the Art of Acting, and the Art of Reciting. Reciting is more difficult than acting. The reciter creates his own atmosphere; he is his own stage manager; he presents the piece and, in a dramatic selection, must play all the parts. He stands alone upon the stage, a thing which, it would seem, the modern actor is incapable of doing, as the author has ceased to entrust him with a soliloquy. For a soliloquy of more than one line, or more frequently of one breath, is nowadays considered technically wrong. The actor is entirely dependent on the author and producer who tell him what to do. The reciter has simply to interpret the author's meaning; to try to intensify his effects by vocal intonation, and appropriate gesture and facial expression. The mimic is independent and unfettered. His province is to form in his own mind an original picture, and to present that picture clearly to his audience. Most mimics are excellent actors. Tate Wilkinson was a notable exception. David Garrick, Edmund Kean, Henry Irving, usurped the province of the author and in every way elevated their art. Samuel Brandram and Clifford Harrison were creative artistes too in the realm of reciting.

The " impressionist " who delivers scene after scene from some heavy play, after the manner of various artistes, is not a real mimic. True mimicry is comedy and burlesque, but certainly not tragedy !

Counterfeit mimics only succeed, as Dr. Johnson said, " of getting out of themselves and not into any one else."

Why these people call themselves " impressionists," I cannot imagine. They, as a rule, make no " impression " on the audience. The bulk of the public fail to see any analogy between their representation and the artiste depicted.

Avoid this parrot-like, phonographic, school of mimicry. Remember that true mimicry is nothing if not creative. It is in fact the most independent of the arts, however " inferior " some may think it. Music appeals to the senses and emotions, and suggests the sister arts poetry and painting—a stage picture with the accompaniment of music and poetry is, as Wagner well knew, alone complete. His music dramas are a perfect blending of music, poetry and painting.

" The craving for mimicry," says Percy Fitzgerald in his interesting biography of Samuel Foote, " has always been found to be irrepressible, and has constantly tended to encroach on the legitimate interests of the stage. It may be said that the origin of our ' music hall ' entertainments is due to the relish for burlesque of the failings and absurdities of our neighbours. A certain indulgence, or even licence, has been extended to this species of enjoyment. There the mimic can revel in spontaneous antics, and draw the attention of a crowded house. . . . Even up to our time there lingered on at taverns such as the Coal Hole and Cider Cellars, a sort of gross entertainment, given while the guests smoked, ate, and drank, such as sham trials at law, etc. At these places some extraordinary perverted talent used to be exhibited. To-day, at the music halls, nothing 'goes down' so well as an imitation of some noted actor, disloyally done by some clever brother.

"There can be no doubt that this drawing from the life, or imitation, not merely of physical defects, and oddities, but of traits of character, becomes under certain conditions of careful study and nice observation a valuable method of producing vivid and dramatic scenes and effects. All the great writers, either in dramas or novels, have used this method, and must use it. Many, either from haste or carelessness, have simply transferred the original to their work, the result being mere recognition of the original. But the genuine masters do not copy line for line or tint for tint. They search for the root or key-note of the character. This they make their own, and play upon it after their own fashion." [1]

It is my endeavour to suggest a practical method for would-be mimics, whose talent is latent and un-

---

[1] Percy Fitzgerald : *Samuel Foote.*

developed, simply through lack of opportunity and encouragement.

First, as I have stated, it is necessary to study the art of acting. Join a good theatrical club; attach yourself to a first-rate dramatic studio—or better still, if you have the time and opportunity, go on the stage. Study the art of acting in all its branches, " voice, speech and gesture." Before you can burlesque an art it is necessary to make yourself well acquainted with it.

Frequent the theatre. If possible, be present at the rehearsals of new productions. Study the plays themselves, and see them gradually grow and develop at every rehearsal. Cultivate your powers of observation both in and out of the theatre.

Learn to think and work logically. The study of logic and psychology will help you very considerably to discover the cause for the various effects you are anxious to produce.

It is necessary to set to work on a good mental basis; to develop your senses, your imagination and will; to train your memory, to study nature. Nature abounds with a thousand pleasant sounds. The rustling of the wind through the leafy trees; the rushing sound of rapid waters; the dash of the cascade; the roar of the ocean and the crash of thunder; the humming bees; the bleating lambs; the song of birds through the silent air. Listen and distinguish them all. Look at the beauties of nature all around; the sunrise at dawn; the sunset at eventide ; and at night, the silvery moon ; and the sky studded with innumerable stars.

Observe the " mimicry of nature." " Insects take the colour of the leaves they feed on. Some moths are mottled so as to mimic the bark of trees, or moss, or the surface of stones. . . . Many harmless animals mimic others which are poisonous. Some butterflies mimic others which are nauseous in taste, and therefore not attacked by birds. In these cases it is generally only the females that are mimetic, and in some cases only a part of them, so that there are two or even three kinds of females, the one retaining the normal colouring of the group, the other mimicking another species. Some spiders closely resemble ants, and several other insects mimic wasps and hornets. Some reptiles and fish have actually the power of changing the colours of their skin so as to adapt themselves to their surroundings. . . . Even the brilliant blue of the kingfisher, which in a museum renders it so conspicuous, in its native haunts, on the contrary, makes it difficult to distinguish from a flash of light upon the water ; and the richly coloured woodpecker wears the genuine dress of a forester—the green coat and crimson cap. . . . In many cases plants mimic others which are better protected than themselves." [1]

Look at nature and notice everything.

" Nature—so full of noises that suggest words,

[1] Sir John Lubbock : *The Beauties of Nature.*

harsh noises of clanging and banging and jingling and jangling, dull noises of rumbling and grumbling, drowsy noises of humming and murmuring, watery noises of dripping and dropping and whirling and swirling and gurgling and rippling, and dashing and splashing; noises through the air; whizzing and whistling and whirring; metallic noises of clinging and ringing; quarrelsome noises of slapping and whacking, knocking and thumping; peculiar noises of sneezing and wheezing; hissing and spitting; plaintive noises of sighing and sobbing, and so on all the day long." [1]

> " All the world is full of music—
>   So at least the wise folks say;
> There is music in the sunshine
>   Such as shines on us to-day:
> Rainbow music in the storm cloud:
>   Flower music in the ground,
> And the harmonies of colour
>   Answering those of song and sound." [2]

---

[1] Philip Gibbs: *Knowledge is Power.*
[2] Clifford Harrison: *On the Common Chords.*

CHAPTER II

Some Celebrated Mimics

L ET us now consider some of the best mimics, past and present.

The greatest actor the English stage has ever seen, David Garrick, was a remarkable mimic.

It is not strange, when we begin to analyse the art of acting, to find that the cleverest actors are invariably the cleverest mimics. The art of acting is the art of impersonating types, as the art of mimicry is the art of impersonating individuals. So, after all, the actor's art is only a modified form of mimicry, and it is not so creative. His province is " to hold the mirror up to nature," whereas the province of the mimic is to dispense with a mirror altogether and present an original effect.

David Garrick, the English Roscius, was born at Hereford 1716.[1] He was educated at Lichfield, where he met Samuel Johnson, with whom he came to London in 1736. In 1741 he first went on the stage, and his success was immediately established. He became the patentee of Drury Lane Theatre in

[1] 19 Feb. 1716-17.

1747 and the remainder of his course, until his retirement in 1776, was one long series of successes. He had wonderful powers of mimicry. Against the vices of style of his contemporary players, he used the most potent of all weapons, ridicule. When playing Bayes in *The Rehearsal* he would check the actors who spoke naturally, and proceed to teach them how to deliver the speeches in true theatrical manner. For this purpose he selected some of the most eminent performers, and assumed the manner and deportment of each in their turn. He would begin with Delane, who, next to Quin, was the leading tragedian of the time. Retiring to the back of the stage, drawing his left arm across his heart, resting his right elbow upon it, and raising a finger to his nose, he would come forward with a stately gait, nodding his head as he advanced, and deliver a speech in the exact tones of this declamatory tragedian. After that, he would proceed to imitate other prominent performers of his day. He never, however, mimicked Quin, whom he considered an excellent actor in parts that suited. him.

David Garrick died on January 20, 1779, and was interred in Westminster Abbey under the monument of Shakespeare.

Samuel Foote, the modern Aristophanes, was born at Truro in Cornwall. He was descended from a very ancient family.

In 1747 he opened a little theatre in the Haymarket, and appeared in a dramatic piece of his own

composing, called the *Diversions of the Morning.*
This piece consisted of the exhibition of several
characters well known in real life, whose style of
conversation and expressions Foote very happily
hit off in the lines of his drama and still more happily
represented on the stage. This performance at
first met with some opposition from the magistrates
at Westminster, as well as from the managers of
Drury Lane playhouse; but the author being
patronized by many of the principal nobility, and
other persons of distinction, the opposition was over-
ruled. Having altered the title of his perfomance,
Foote proceeded without further molestation, to
give *Tea in a Morning* to his friends, and represented it through a run of forty mornings to crowded
and splendid audiences.

Foote acquainted the spectators that he was training some young performers for the stage, he would
with their permission, whilst tea was being prepared,
proceed with his instructions before them. He then
commenced a series of ludicrous imitations of the
players, who, one and all, became exceedingly
exasperated against him. Few amusements were
ever so popular.

The ensuing season he produced another piece of
the same kind which he called *The Auction of
Pictures.* This piece also had a very great run.
His *Knights,* the produce of the following season,
was a performance of somewhat more dramatic
regularity; but still, although his plot and characters

seemed less immediately personal, it was apparent that he kept some real characters strongly in his eye in the performance ; and the town took upon themselves to fix them where the resemblance seemed to be most striking.

One of Foote's most famous caricatures was Mr. Cadwallader in *The Author*. The original of this character was an intimate friend of his, a Welsh gentleman named Ap-Rice, (or Apreece) an enormously corpulent person, with a broad staring face, an incoherent way of speaking, a loud voice, an awkward gait, a trick of rolling his head from side to side, and of sucking his wrists.   Here was a splendid subject for the mimic, and he produced him to the life, to the huge delight of the audience, among which more than once was to be found Apreece himself, who, in happy ignorance that he was gazing on his own reflection, laughed as loudly and applauded as vigorously as anybody.   But it was impossible that he should long remain in this blissful ignorance, for so unmistakable was the imitation to everybody but the victim, that he could not enter a coffee-room or be seen in any public place, without people whispering " There's Cadwallader ! " ; or some one calling after him " This is my Becky, my dear Becky " ; one of the phrases in the play.   When the Welshman at length realized the fact, he was furious, and obtained an injunction from the Lord Chamberlain to restrain the performance.

Dr. Johnson said of Foote : " The first time

I was in company with Foote, I was resolved not to be pleased—and it is very difficult to please a man against his will. I went on eating my dinner pretty sullenly, affecting for a long time not to mind him, but the dog was so very comical that I was obliged to lay down my knife and fork, throw myself back on my chair, and fairly laugh it out with the rest : there was no avoiding it—the fellow was irresistible."

Tate Wilkinson was born October 27, 1739. He was a pupil of Samuel Foote and was so remarkable a mimic that he could reproduce even the face of a beautiful woman. His fame as an actor was very slight otherwise. He was engaged by Garrick for Drury Lane, but was only cast for the smallest parts. Foote, however, having entertained a good opinion of him, engaged him for Ireland, where he appeared in Mr. Foote's *Tea* with so much success, that the then Irish manager, Mr. Sheridan, engaged him on a salary of three guineas per week. Notwithstanding, on his return to London, he was still discouraged and slighted by Mr. Garrick : but during a summer season he had an opportunity of appearing at Bath, where he appeared in *Othello* and treated Mr. Foote with a dish of his own tea. He not only mimicked the actors who were distinguished in his day, but Foote's manner of imitating them. He published several works on Theatrical History. Though nothing as an actor, and too self-important as a writer, he was a genius as a mimic, and a very zealous friend of the stage ; highly respected as a manager both by the performers and public. He died in 1803.

Wilkinson was powerless when attempting to mimic the voice and manner of Mrs. Cibber. The tone, manner and method of Garrick, Foote, Luke, Sparks, Barry, Mrs. Bellamy, Mrs. Crawford, Mrs. Woffington, he could reproduce with wonderful approach to exactness. But Mrs. Cibber's excellence baffled him He remembered her, and it, but he could not do more than remember. " It is all in my mind's eye," he would say, with a sigh, at his incapacity.

Charles Mathews was born on June 28, 1776, and was educated in London. His father was a bookseller and intended his son to follow the same profession, but his early inclination for the stage overcame parental counsel and he made his first appearance as an amateur—curiously enough in the part of Richard III—at the Richmond Theatre in 1793, as a professional comedian in the Theatre Royal, Dublin, the following year. He was a wonderful master of personification and mimicry, and while mimicking every one, he never lost a friend, or hurt the feelings of the most sensitive. His taste was as instinctive as his wit. His wonderful variety of facial expression and his gentlemanly sarcasm were long remembered after his death His son Charles also achieved a brilliant reputation in the same line.

Mathews the elder had many imitators in his own line, but never an equal. To judge by the stories related by Mrs. Mathews, his powers of mimicry, or rather of transformation, must have been nothing less than marvellous, for, without make up, change of dress or any stage trickery, he could change his personality so as to deceive his most intimate friends. He was once expelled from behind the scenes of the Liverpool Theatre, where he was actually playing at the time, as an intrusive stranger; and the next moment, after simply allowing his features and figure to assume their normal appearance, passed through the stage door again, and was recognized as Mr. Mathews. In those days the habitués of the boxes had the entrée of the Green Room of Drury Lane; among those who availed themselves of the privilege was a curious old gentleman of the name of Pennyman, and whose behaviour was so eccentric that he soon became a notorious character. No one could tell how the gentleman got admittance, and therefore there was no mode of excluding him. Every night he attracted inconvenient numbers to the Green Room.

One night in the middle of a greater excitement than usual, he suddenly stood before the assembled crowd as Mr. Mathews.

When Godwin was writing *Cloudesley*, he asked Mathews to furnish him with some hints upon the possibilities of disguise. Mathews invited him to dinner, and after the meal was over gave him some ocular demonstrations upon the subject. Presently, while his guest was conversing with Mrs. Mathews,

the host slipped out of the room, and, almost immediately afterwards, a servant entered to announce a
Mr. Jenkins. He was introduced to Mr. Godwin, and
began to talk so incessantly about that gentleman's
works and made such impertinent inquiries concerning the forthcoming one, that the illustrious author,
bored and annoyed, rose from his seat and went to
the window that opened on to the lawn : but Mr.
Jenkins was not so easily evaded. He pushed
before him and officiously offered to open the
window ; after fumbling a little he threw it open
and turned round ; then, to his astonishment,
Godwin saw another man—not Mr. Jenkins, but
Charles Mathews.

When Mathews imitated Lord Ellenborough,
he received a polite request from his lordship not to
repeat it. He respected this intimation, although his
refusal to comply with the demand of a crowded
house next night, which had been drawn by the
report of this wonderful mimicry, almost caused a
riot. The Prince Regent, however, sent for him to
Carlton House, and commanded the imitation, over
which His Royal Highness went into ecstasies of
admiration. After this, Mathews became, a terror
to judges and barristers, whenever he was seen in
court. One day, while on a provincial tour, he
strolled into the sessions-house at Shrewsbury during
a trial. Presently an usher came to him with the
judge's compliments to enquire if he would like a
seat upon the bench. Rather astonished, as he had

no acquaintance with his lordship, Mathews followed his conductor and was most effusively received. Relating the incident some years afterwards, to a legal friend, he was commenting on the politeness shown him, when the listener burst out laughing.

"I've heard the judge tell the story," he said, "and I remember him saying, 'I was so frightened when I caught sight of that d——d Mathews in the court with his eyes upon me, that I couldn't fix my thoughts upon the case, for I believe he had come there for the purpose of taking me off on the stage that night, so I thought it was best to be as civil to him as possible.'"

Once when taking off a brother actor, he suddenly saw that he was present in the theatre. Greatly shocked, he affectionately apologized "My dear friend, did you mean *that* for me?" said the actor. "Don't distress yourself, there was not the least likeness!"

In Foote's day, mimicry was a recognized accomplishment. In social life an "agreeable rattle" who could "take off" a well-known acquaintance, was in much demand. Dr. Johnson spoke with praise of a well known London lady who excelled in mimicry. "I believe," he added, "she has now gone mad!"

It is well known that George IV., a prince of many accomplishments, was an incomparable mimic, and used to convulse his friends by taking off his own Ministers, foreign visitors, and others, in the most humorous and lifelike fashion.

In Edinburgh there was a famous mimic, Dr. Cullen, who is mentioned by Boswell. His reputation as such was truly extraordinary. Dugald Steward declared that " he was the most perfect of all mimics." Lord Cockburn says that he could copy not only the looks, tones, peculiarities, etc., but " the very words—nay the very thoughts—of his subjects."

George Alexander Stevens used to give a very clever original performance. He had prepared a number of modelled heads representing many types —politicians, writers, players, etc., on which he commented in a very satirical and amusing way. Both Foote and Mathews had the miraculous faculty of thinking or speaking upon a given subject exactly as that person himself would think or speak.

John Reeve gave imitations of contemporary actors in *The Life of an Actor*, produced September 4, 1824.

Gustave Doré is said to have been a perfect mimic, being able to accurately reproduce the gestures and expressions of a person speaking by his side.

John Parry was an inimitable mimic and entertainer. He inspired Corney Grain, and afterwards George Grossmith, to give musical sketches at the piano. He prefaced his sketches with a medley of all the popular tunes of the day, operatic and otherwise. In his line he was nothing less than a genius— now, alas, almost entirely forgotten.

George Grossmith, Clifford Harrison, Albert

Chevalier, were wonderfully good mimics of types. Unfortunately the German Reed and Corney Grain style of entertainment died with them. They have left the world poorer—by a smile.

Corney Grain presented to his audiences a series of vivid pictures ; the Precocious School-boy—the Sporting Undergraduate—the Doctor of Divinity—Dear Mamma—'Arry by the Sea—the British Matron —the Wealthy Parvenu—French and German types —Mrs. Grundy and her near relations—the Prig—Smart and Suburban Society—Imitations of various instruments in an orchestra—the Bull Dog and the Fat Baby, a specimen of some patent food, etc.

When we look around to-day, visit theatres, music halls, concerts, and see inferior talent everywhere, it is a treat to enter the Apollo, and to be able to laugh heartily at the great Pelissier, and his clever company of Follies. There you see true burlesque, and the revival of many a lost art. Pelissier is a Corney Grain, Gilbert and Sullivan rolled into one, which may account for his robust rotundity ! Like Corney Grain, he is a born impersonator of types. He has the true spirit of burlesque. His *Potted Plays* are little gems of their kind. The embryo mimic cannot do better than visit the Follies, as frequently as possible, and there breathe the atmosphere of irresponsible fantasy and true burlesque. There he will have the opportunity of studying the methods of that admirable mimic Morris Harvey, and he could not possibly have a better model, for Mr. Morris Harvey is quick, clever, and alert. How rapidly he changes his voice, and seizes on the salient points of his various victims. He is fortunate in being under the sway of such a crertive artiste as his chief, who must be a great help to him in originating ideas and working out his effects.

If you wish to see artistes at their best and enjoy a unique and inimitable entertainment you must visit the Savage Club some Saturday night. Of course these evenings vary like everything else. Sometimes the talent presented may be mediocre; but the assembly is always courteous; well knowing the best material, and being themselves experts in some branch of art or science, they are tolerant. The bohemian atmosphere is a kindly one. The spirit of charity, humanity, wit, cosmopolitanism, and generosity that abounds in the Savage Club is as refreshing as it is rare.

One of the best of Savages, the cheeriest of creatures, and the most facile of mimics, is Arthur Helmore. He hits off the peculiarities of a host of clerics He has made the demeanour of divines his special study, and has magnified their characteristics in a genial and kindly way. His performance is entirely without offence. He is equally happy in his impersonations of all the prominent actors and actresses of the day. These sketches are humorous and diverting imageries of well known people, and in them his own genial and critical nature is evident.

They are never marred by an uncharitable note; they are the outcome of a benevolent and deeply religious temperament.

Bransby Williams is well known to the music hall public, and a great favourite. He is a keen observer, and an impersonator of very great power. The characters of Charles Dickens are presented with marvellous fidelity and emphasis. His long music hall experience has accustomed him to lay on his effects with rather a heavy hand. He is perfectly right. It is useless to try to be subtle in a large music hall; you will only succeed in being unintelligible, which may " go down " in the case of a great artiste; for the public follow public opinion as a rule, like a flock of sheep; and whether they understand or not, they usually applaud a star. Mr. Bransby Williams' delineation of Dickens types are so popular that he doesn't favour the public with his imitations of mimes as often as we should like. He certainly is a most talented delineator of a large number of fellow artistes. Perhaps his impersonations are the most lifelike and truthful of any living mimic. But then he is a careful student, a very hard worker, and he has had a long and wide experience.

Cyril Clensy is a young mimic who has come to the front very quickly. He has scored several great successes at the Palace, and elsewhere. He thoroughly deserves his popularity, for he is extremely versatile and clever. His facial expressions are always true to the artiste he is depicting, and he is swiftly making the most rapid progress in his art.

The best known actor-mimics are Arthur Playfair, Seymour Hicks, Farren Soutar, and Gerald du Maurier. They are all extremely clever actors.

Poor Arthur Faber and Rob Harwood ! They were both clever mimics. Arthur Faber's impressions were wonderfully striking portraits of various widely different types. Both of these talented artistes were deservedly popular, and were courted and entertained in bohemian circles—sometimes too brilliantly ! Probably if they had lived in some other country, where art is not merely an accidental, but a thing as wonderful and as welcome as the sun that shines, they would have gained a greater measure of renown. For, in this solemn isle, great artistes seldom laurels win.

Smith Wright, a cultured and remarkable mimic, seems to have disappeared. His entertainments were most original. His impersonations were faithful and humorous portraits. There was a subtlety and charm about his work that has never been duly appreciated.

Donald Calthrop, son of John Clayton, and nephew of Dion Boucicault, should have a brilliant career. He is a clever mimic, and very ambitious and youthful.

Miss Cissie Loftus, and Miss Marie Dainton, are both very good actresses and vocalists. The Folly ladies—Miss Gwennie Mars, and Miss Ethel Allandale—are wonderfully clever and charming. Their impersonations are truthful and artistic.

Miss Alice Pierce, Miss Marie Mansfield, Miss Nina Gordon and Miss Valli Valli are very popular with the music hall public.

There are countless minor mimics. I cannot yield to the temptation of increasing the bulk of this volume by recording their praises. They are most of them painstaking and energetic, and their numbers are daily increasing.

READINGS :

Dr. Doran's *Annals of the English Stage. The London Stage*, by Barton Baker. *Memoirs of Charles Mathews, Romance of the English Stage*, and *Samuel Foote*, by Percy Fitzgerald. *Lives of Eminent Englishmen, Thespian Dictionary*, and Tate Wilkinson's Memoirs. R. W. Lowe's *English Theatrical Literature.*

c

CHAPTER III

First Principles

IT is only by analysing that we arrive at the first principles of any art or science. The majority of people never take the trouble to analyse, consequently their ideas and arguments remain fixed and engrained in their minds ; and they never advance any further in the sphere of thought. It is this faculty of analysing that enables a man to think dispassionately ; it is the secret of success in any profession.

We have seen that the sage of the eighteenth century, Dr. Johnson, considered that to be a good mimic requires " great powers " ;—" great acuteness of observation " ;—" great retention of what is observed " ;—and " great pliancy of organs to represent what is observed." In other words, to be a good mimic we must cultivate our powers of observation and concentration. They are certainly " great powers " which can be cultivated only by constant practice. " Pliancy of organs to represent what is observed " can, to a certain extent, be developed by vocal and physical exercises.

By the process of analysis Dr. Johnson discovered the first principles of the Art of Mimicry. It is only by cultivating these principles that we can advance in this art.

1. "*Acuteness of Observation.*"—Get in the habit of noticing everything, not only in the theatre, but in the smallest matters of everyday life. Notice the little details in or out of doors. Let nothing, however small, escape you.

In watching the performance of an experienced mimic, you notice he brings out all the smallest peculiarities of his subjects with a vividness of detail that is entirely absent in the performance of some precocious amateur.

The facial expression, the characteristic movement, the favourite gesture, the psychological pause, the monotonous intonation, the infectious laugh, the blinking eye, the workings of the mouth, the open or closed tone, the upward inflection, the sigh, the marked modulation, or monotonous cadence, the minor key, the fall into thirds or fifths, the vibrato stop, the pitch, the mouthings, the "ranting" and "sawing of the air," the mighty crescendo, the diminuendo, the method of the melodramatic hero—who lets it "rip"—the emphasis, and last, but not least, the "little touches" are all to be observed, and faithfully recorded.

You can only obtain good effects by the habit of closely noticing everything from every point of view. You must realize everything at the theatre.

You must place yourself in the position of the various performers and the audience, note the effect a certain striking piece of acting has upon the audience, and find out the cause of its popularity. Realize both the actor, and the author's responsibility for a telling effect.

There is a story of two knights who met together on opposite sides of a monument. One of them praised the gold on the shield of the warrior sculptured upon it, and the other answered that it was not gold but silver. On this issue they fought; and, in the course of the combat, they changed places and were flung each upon the ground occupied originally by his foe. Then they discovered that the shield was gold on one side, silver on the other, and that both of them were right, and both were wrong.

Yet in the habit of entering into the feelings and emotions of actors, authors, and audience, and judging dispassionately, cultivate your faculties of observation, concentration and comparison in and out of the theatre. Don't let any of your powers deteriorate from want of use.

Most people go about half their time with their eyes closed. Dr. Johnson expressed his dissatisfaction at Boswell not observing the different objects on the road. " If I had your eyes," he said, " I would count the passengers."

Decide on a certain subject that you wish to include in your repertoire, some prominent actor with a strongly marked personality. Mark his movements,

facial expression, and gestures. Never mind the
other people on the stage ; notice him alone. Never
mind his voice at first, try and catch his movements ;
then fix his intonations. Begin by trying to reproduce his walk, gestures and facial expression.
Having fixed them, now try to reproduce his voice.
Never mind the words he utters ; try to fix the tone,
and discover by the ear agreement, or disagreement.
It is very necessary to cultivate the senses.

You must commence gradually ; adding detail
upon detail ; until, after continual elaboration, you
evolve a vivid representation of all the peculiarities
of your subject.

2. *" Great retention of what is observed."* This is
the second of the canons of Mimicry expounded by
Dr. Johnson.

If you wish to retain anything, (1) impress it once
for all indelibly on your mind, (2) compare it with
some similar things, (3) bring all your senses to
bear upon it.

The faculty of retentiveness comes under the
great law of Association of Ideas, which is the secret
of training the memory. Memorizing consists in
fixing your attention so closely on your subject that
you can reproduce the impression with ease. But
in order to reproduce the mind cannot be too firmly
fixed in the first instance. This faculty can only
be acquired by frequent practice. The more we
think as a rule the less we observe and vice versâ.

Our recollections succeed one another, not arbitrarily, but according to certain laws. Psychologists have reduced them to a few general principles which have been called the Association of Ideas.

(1) The law of similarity.

(2) The law of contrast.

(3) The law of contiguity.

(1) A photo recalls the original. Painting, sculpture, the drama are similar, and suggest certain figures and scenes that we afterwards associate with these arts.

(2) Wealth recalls poverty. Cold suggests heat ; virtue, vice, and so on.

(3) The law of contiguity teaches that the mind in the presence of an object or event, whether actual or ideal, tends to recall other objects, and events, formerly closely connected in space or time with that now present.

The phrase " Association of Ideas " has played an important part in the history of English philosophy, and has been recognized as a principle governing the faculty of recollection and retentiveness from the time of Aristotle.

" Reminiscence," says Aristotle, " takes place in virtue of the constitution of our mind, whereby each mental movement is determined to arise as the sequel of a certain other."

Philip Gibbs on the subject of the " science of mind " says : " I look in a jeweller's shop, and see a string of pearls. I immediately think of Queen Elizabeth, who was so fond of that gem, my thoughts then fly to Haddon Hall where I saw Elizabeth's bedroom two summers ago ; that reminds me how a crowd of Cockney tourists disturbed my pleasure by their facetious rowdiness, and I find myself wishing that the English language were better taught in the London Board schools. From that reflection, I pass on to a consideration of the new Education Bill for London. Now unless this Association of Ideas were traced out step by step, it would at first seem impossible that the sight of a string of pearls should cause me to ponder over an Education Bill ! " [1]

Everything grows by progressive stages. One thing leads to another. Little by little an effect is produced. The process involves many struggles and failures, from there being so much in it depending on accidental circumstances. Getting in the habit of noticing everything, especially details, is the royal road to success in the art of mimicry.

Nothing is more difficult at rehearsal than the small details in a play. A servant enters with a letter and delivers it to one of the characters. " Where does he enter ? " cries the stage manager. " He enters right," replies Snooks, his assistant. " He can't come on right," says the stage manager, " it means re-arranging that group up stage. He must come on left." " He can't come on left," says Snooks, " he would encounter Lady Pimple, who comes on immediately." " Hang Lady Pimple," says the

[1] Philip Gibbs : *Facts and Ideas.*

stage manager, "she had better appear at the centre opening." "There is no centre opening in this act." "Good heavens! well—let's get on with it! What is the cue?" Snooks has been so occupied in thinking out the situation that for the moment he cannot find the place. The stage manager, getting impatient, snatches the manuscript from Snooks, at the same time knocking his knee against a chair. He utters the usual epithet, and drops the "script." He and Snooks try to pick it up at the same time, and bang their heads together. Then the stage manager relapses into blank verse, and both men snarl at one another! It is decided that the servant must enter right, and the whole grouping of the stage is re-arranged. They go through the entrance again to fix it, and the stage manager gives the cue. The servant, a very nervous young actor, doesn't appear.

"Lionel Kingsley," shouts the stage manager, "it is your cue—now hurry up—Come on with the letter." "I haven't got it!" "Oh, hang it! Why not?—Where is it?" "You had it last," answers Lionel. "I had!" exclaims the stage manager. "I gave it to you Snooks." "I gave it to Props," says Snooks. "Oh, never mind. Let us run through the scene without it." They go through it again, and proceed with the dialogue; and the very next speech necessitates the re-grouping of the stage. Two of the characters ought to be together, and the stage manager has put them on opposite sides of the stage ! He rearranges them, and they go back again. After several repetitions—each of which produces further complications—the scene is fixed. Every one is out of temper. The leading lady pitches into the author, who pitches into the assistant stage manager, who pitches into the nervous Lionel Kingsley; who, thoroughly worn out, wishes his salary was more than two guineas a week. Then he goes out and has a drink.

I have dwelt on this mental picture in order to impress upon you the value of details. It is the retention of a succession of small details that denotes the great artiste. It is the most essential thing in the training of the embryo mimic. Attend to little details and the bigger things will look after themselves.

Learn to discriminate. Be very careful that nothing in your performance is calculated to give offence. Never be personal and uncharitable, or you will quickly degenerate into a mere buffoon. Remember there is always the unwritten law of good taste. Learn a lesson from this fable : " The man once invited the lion to be his guest and received him with princely hospitality. The lion had the run of a magnificent palace, in which there were a vast many things to admire. There were large saloons and long corridors, richly furnished and decorated, and filled with a profusion of fine specimens of sculpture and painting, the works of the first masters in either art. The subjects represented were various ; but the most prominent of them had an especial interest for the noble animal who stalked by them. It was that of the lion himself ; and as the owner of the mansion led him from one apartment into another, he did not fail to direct his attention to the indirect homage which these various groups and tableaux paid to the importance of the lion tribe.

" There was, however, one remarkable feature in all of them, to which the host, silent as he was from politeness, seemed not at all insensible ; that diverse as were these representations, in one point of view they all agreed, that the man was always victorious, and the lion was always overcome. The man had it all his own way, and the lion was but a fool, and served to make him sport. There were exquisite works in marble of Samson rending the lion like a kid, and young David taking the lion by the beard, and choking him. There was the man who ran his arm down the lion's throat and held him fast by the tongue ; and there was that other who, when carried off in his teeth, contrived to pull a penknife from his pocket, and lodge it in the monster's heart. Then there was a lion hunt, or what had been such, for the brute was rolling round in the agonies of death, and his conqueror on his bleeding horse was surveying these from a distance.

" There was a gladiator from the Roman amphitheatre in mortal struggle with his tawny foe, and it was plain who was getting the mastery. There was a lion in a net ; a lion in a trap ; four lions, yoked in harness, were drawing the car of a Roman emperor ; and elsewhere stood Hercules, clad in the lion's skin, and with the club which demolished him.

" Nor was this all : the lion was not only triumphed over, mocked, spurned ; but he was tortured into extravagant forms, as if he were not only the slave and creature, but the very creation of man. He became an artistic decoration, and an heraldic emblazonment. The feet of alabaster tables fell away into lions' paws. Lions' faces grinned on either side the shining mantelpiece ; and lions' mouths held tight the handles of the doors. There were sphinxes, too, half lion half woman ; there were lions rampant holding flags, lions couchant, lions passant, lions regardant ; lions and unicorns ; there were lions white, black and red : in short there was no misconception, or excess of indignity which was thought too great for the lord of the forest, and the king of brutes. After he had gone over the mansion, his entertainer asked him what he thought of the splendours it contained ; and he in reply did full justice to the riches of its owner, and the skill of its decorators, but he added, ' Lions would have fared better, had lions been the artists.' "[1]

Learn to look at everything from every point of view, to analyse, and judge dispassionately. Think

[1] John Henry Newman : *Protestant View of the Catholic Church.*

for yourself and don't be guided always by second-hand opinions.

3. " *Great pliancy of organs to represent what is observed.*" This faculty is common to great singers, actors and reciters as well as to good mimics.

To acquire this " pliancy " it is necessary to study the first principles of acting and singing. That is why I so strongly recommend going on the stage. It is also necessary to take some lessons in voice production from some qualified professor such as Mr Watkin Mills.   .

Don't rely on voice lozenges, raw eggs or stimulants. The best recipe is to keep in good physical condition, take plenty of exercise and you can practise breathing exercises at home. There are several : a good specialist would advise you on the subject. Don't go to some acrobat, boxer, heavy weight lifter, or wrestler. They are mostly quacks. You must work on a sound, scientific basis.

An excellent breathing exercise, that you cannot too frequently practise, is to place the right foot forward. Lean back, extend your arms, with hands open straight in front of you. Gradually draw in your breath through the nostrils and slowly extend your arms above your head ; then as far back as possible ; and gradually outwards, and downwards to the sides ; while at the same time, exhale freely. Repeat a score of times, morning, and night, and during the day.

No one can speak well who is not master of the art

of respiration. My uncle the late E. O. Bleackley in his Essay on *Effective Reading*, published in 1881, said, " Although I do not believe Elocution is an art that can be taught, yet I consider that by its rules, a poor speaker may be made into a more effective one—that he may learn to control his voice and to save his breath for the powerful passages, and thus cause his delivery to be impressive, and commanding. But, as in singing, nature alone can give the harmonious tones, the tender pathos, the impassioned fire of the finished elocutionist." [1]

My uncle was a very excellent reciter. He had a magnificent voice. He also gave imitations of eminent actors including Charles Kean, Charles Pitt, Charles Matthews, Charles Fechter, G. V. Brooke, J. B. Buckstone, and Signor Salvini. In August 1860, when the Savage Club was visiting Manchester, in order to give a performance at the Theatre Royal for the benefit of the Robert Brough Testimonial Fund, my uncle recited the prologue which the late Charles Swain undertook to write.

Although many are of the opinion that elocution cannot be taught, yet it is astonishing what can be done by application and development.

Demosthenes, the greatest orator of Greece, conquered the physical disadvantages under which he laboured. His health was naturally feeble, his voice harsh and tuneless and his action ungraceful.

[1] E. O. Bleackley : *Effective Reading.*

To strengthen his lungs he used to climb steep hills, reciting as he went, or declaim on the shores of the sea in stormy weather. To improve his delivery he took instructions from Satyrus the actor, and did not even disdain to study effects from a mirror. His feebleness of health he never fairly overcame, but he obviated the defects of his early training by the severest study pursued for months at a time without an interruption. He became the prince of ancient orators.

Daily practise the " Solfeggio " and the " Messa di voce." Run up and down the scales, singing the monosyllables, Do, Re, Mi, etc.

All tones should be preceded by inhalation. The inspirations should be noiseless. If the chest is raised, with both passages to the lungs open, the air will enter silently and instantaneously. The breath should be taken through the nostrils. The freest respiration is obtained by using both passages, although inhalation through the nostrils alone is preferable. The outward impulse which the air receives in speech should be given, not so much by descent of the thorax or walls of the chest, as by ascent of diaphragm, or base of the chest.

Study nature in all its phases. Pay close attention to everything. Avoid stimulants and practise vocal and physical exercises daily.

If you take an interest in the work of gradually following out the hints I have ventured to offer, I am sure you will soon be surprised at the rapid

progress you have made in an art which has had
comparatively few followers, and which is generally
considered to be a natural gift, which cannot possibly
be cultivated.

CHAPTER IV

The Senses

IT is only by training the senses that we can possess the spirit of observation, concentrated attention, and a penetration that find close resemblances.

The Australian bushman, by a footprint in the dust, can tell who has passed, and how long ago. The Red Indian observes anything unusual in the forest, and can, at a great distance, hear the remotest sound.

By training the senses our retentiveness increases. All persons are not alike susceptible to the growth of new powers, or as regards all subjects. A much greater degree of practice is necessary in one case than in the other, and a constant striving to observe the laws of health and to preserve freshness and vigour. " The special portions of the organism endowed with the property of reacting to certain stimuli are called sense-organs." [1]

Each sense has its own office, and must be separately trained. " The senses allow of a certain amount

[1] Fr. Maher : *Psychology*.

of substitution one for the other, but each has its special function, which cannot be replaced by any of the others." [1]

We really understand very little about our senses. Take the question of colour. The rainbow is commonly said to consist of seven colours : red, orange, yellow, green, blue, indigo and violet ; but it is now known that all our colour sensations are mixtures of three single colours—red, green and violet. We are quite ignorant how we perceive these colours.

Take the sense of hearing. The vibrations of the air no doubt play upon the drum of the ear, and the waves thus produced are conducted through a chain of tiny bones to the *fenestra ovatis*, and so to the inner ear, or *labyrinth*. " When we pass on to the senses of smell and taste, all we know is that the extreme nerve fibres terminate in certain cells which differ in form from those of the general surface, but in what manner the innumerable differences of taste and smell are communicated to the brain we are absolutely ignorant." [2]

Accustom yourself to compare different types and to associate your ideas in the way that I have suggested. At the same time train your senses daily. In time you will find yourself paying closer attention to everything. As you are gradually able to fix impressions more closely in your mind, and, by

[1] Edridge Green : *Memory and its Cultivation.*
[2] Sir John Lubbock : *Beauties of Nature.*

continual practice, to reproduce them with more or less facility, your interest and sense-perception will be greatly stimulated.

Learn to classify types. Emerson says : " The difference between men is in their principle of association. Some men classify objects by colour, and size ; others by accidents of appearance ; others by intrinsic likeness, or by the relation of cause and effect. The progress of the intellect consists in the clearer vision of causes which overlooks surface differences." [1]

The training of the senses is the true basis of the Art of Mimicry. The first step therefore is to train your senses daily.

A continual practice of the sense of hearing will enable you to perceive more and more quickly the agreements in the tones of various voices, and, by carefully classifying them, and noticing minute differences of certain tones you can gradually fix in your mind vivid impressions, which continual practice will enable you to reproduce with more or less facility.

You visit a theatre and listen attentively to the tones of a certain actor's voice. His methods and delivery make a distinct impression on you, so that the very next day when you attend, let us say, the Law Courts, you are struck with the similarity between the actor's voice, and the learned K.C., who is stating his case. The following day you listen to a

---

[1] Emerson : *Essays.*

celebrated preacher and you are impressed with his delivery and are constantly reminded of the actor and the barrister whom you have just heard. Make a study of these three subjects who have so much in common ; and, after a time, by noticing the difference of their respective personalities, you will be able to develop three separate impressions ; and thus practically to kill three birds with one stone. Notice that the barrister, accustomed to address his Lordship, will pitch his voice up, whilst the preacher, accustomed to address his congregation, will perhaps be more constrained and direct his voice downwards. The actor will use more gesture and modulation than the others, as his part by constant practice has become a fixed oration. The study of the three different types will strengthen your impressions. Lose no opportunity of listening to them as often as possible. This is the great method of Association of Ideas which is so valuable in acquiring the Art of Mimicry.

External objects manifest themselves to the mind through the senses. " If a person of average ability directly after having looked at a picture or a photograph, close his eyes and think of that picture, the remembrance of it will be almost as vivid as the sensory impression itself ; if the observer had waited for a minute or two before trying to think of the picture the remembrance would have been less vivid."[1]

[1] Edridge Green : *Memory*.

Try to fix your impressions when they are fresh in the mind. Don't attempt too much at first, but gradually elaborate your ideas. Never cease to exercise the senses, to associate your ideas, to classify types and peculiarities, to compare character with character, to notice everything.

" The wise man's eyes are in his head," says Solomon, " but the fool walketh in darkness."

After all many people will think, if a person has never shown any special aptitude for the Art of Mimicry, it will be so much labour in vain to practise it. This is not true in every case. With many the faculty may be latent. They only need a guide and a little perseverance.

Sir Joshua Reynolds was such a believer in the force of industry that he held that excellence in art, "however expressed by genius, taste, or the gift of heaven, may be acquired." Writing to Barry he said, " Whoever is resolved to excel in painting, or indeed any other art, must bring all his mind to bear upon that one object from the moment that he rises till he goes to bed."

Those who are altogether devoid of art, who are awkward and *gauche*, who never succeeded in anything but making money, and browbeating their neighbour, condemn the followers of an art which they are singularly incapable of pursuing themselves ; on account perhaps of their limited powers of analysis, sense-perception and imagination. " Minds in different states and circumstances cannot under-

stand one another," says Newman in his *Apologia*—
"Children do not apprehend the thoughts of grown
up people, nor savages the instincts of civilization,
nor blind men the perceptions of sight, nor pagans
the doctrines of Christianity, nor men the experi-
ences of Angels. In the same way, there are people
of matter-of-fact, prosaic minds, who cannot take
in the fancies of poets ; and others of shallow, in-
accurate minds, who cannot take in the ideas of
philosophical inquirers." [1]

We find persons giving their fellows lectures in
good taste, manners, and propriety, clad in a frock
coat, top hat, and brown shoes in the country.
They have no sense of humour.

In noticing the peculiarities of various individuals
and finding qualities you may dislike in him, don't
ignore yourself, but practise a little introspection
and discover your own little short-comings and try
to correct them. This may cause you to be more
charitable.

"Our knowledge of the external world is all
based on impressions conveyed to the brain by the
sensory nerves, which convey a large number of
impressions that are included under the names of
the special senses, sight, hearing, smell, touch and
taste." [2]

Every one of these senses must be properly developed if we are to advance in our art. In studying

[1] J. H. Newman : *Apologia.*
[2] Edridge Green : *Memory.*

the history of the stage it is sad to find so many
talented artistes deteriorate through the abuse of
the sense of taste.   Intemperance has been the ruin
of hundreds of clever exponents of the drama.   The
other senses suffer if one is abused, as well as the
imagination, the intellect, the heart, the body and the
soul.

"The sense of hearing introduces to us innumerable delights.   Nature abounds with pleasing
sounds given obviously for man's gratification,
no less than for the purposes of utility.

"The sense of seeing introduces the mind into an
almost unbounded area of enjoyment, especially
when the eye is educated to observe those charming
combinations of light, colour and form which are
generally summed up in the word 'beauty.'   All
nature and art invite us to partake of this pleasure.
In the sky from morning till eve there are atmo-
spheric effects charming the attentive spectator.
Who, that has seen it, could forget sunrise on the
Rigi, or mid-day at Windermere, when mountain
and cloud are fused together in one indistinguish-
able blaze of glory.   Moon, stars and meteors are
words that recall visions of loveliness more subdued
than those afforded by the king of day, but not less
beautiful.   The sea again has its store of beauty.
So with Nature's workmanship on land.   Each leaf
and plant and tree rightly studied is a separate
work of glory from the tiny moss to the spreading
palm. . . .   The possessor of an educated eye finds

in nature everywhere a feast of loveliness provided for him.

" The *perceptive* powers of the mind yield, when properly opened up, an ample store of pleasure. Through the medium of the senses the perceptive faculty is brought acquainted with various objects, all more or less calculated to gratify an inquiring spirit. A habit of observation is necessary, however, and this habit is what many individuals are too lazy to form, going as they do through life with their eyes sealed up, as it were, in a bag." [1]

If you wish to acquire the power of observation, perception, concentration and comparison, exercise your senses daily, and lead a healthy, active life.

Great artistes are invariably sensitive and nervous. This sensitiveness is due to the extreme conscientiousness, susceptibility and discernment which they have cultivated. Power is only another name for nervous force. Owing to their training and talents actors have a considerable amount of feeling, emotion, magnetism and sensibility, because they have fully developed their sense-perception. Hence the artistic temperament.

[1] W. Haigh Miller : *The Culture of Pleasure.*

CHAPTER V

The Memory

WE will suppose that you have put into practice the first principles of the Art of Mimicry, and have been carefully training your senses ; that you have been visiting the theatre with the object of studying various types and well-known figures ; that you have been careful of your mode of life, and have endeavoured to store up the greatest amount of nerve-force by being moderate in all things ; that you have taken a wholesome amount of physical and vocal exercise ; that you have accustomed yourself to let none of the details of everyday life escape you ; that you have been training your ear by listening to the varieties of sounds all around you, especially to the human voice ; that you have been working systematically and not erratically and haphazard.

Artistes as a rule either overwork themselves and utterly exhaust their energies and nervous force, or go to the other extreme and let day after day pass by, whilst they are lost in reverie.

We will suppose you have analysed, associated

your ideas, classified, compared and established a system, and what has been the result of it all ? You have found to your great surprise and edification that, whereas, a short time ago, you were unobservant and lethargic, now you see clearly and swiftly ; that your sense perception is remarkably acute, as well as your sense of humour ; for it stands to reason that if your other senses are being quickened, that subtle, and, in many cases, very latent sense of humour is quickened too.

One of the greatest surprises in your mental, vocal and physical development, will be the great improvement in your health and general state of mind. You will find that your memory has become better, quicker and stronger. It is of the greatest possible importance to possess a good memory, and nothing will strengthen and quicken it like the practice of mimicry. In fact the great Dr. Johnson, as we have seen, has associated mimicry and memory together. He has shown us that this art requires " great retention." Nothing is more valuable than a retentive memory.

" In men like Macaulay (who, as Sydney Smith said, was a library in breeches) and Whewell of Cambridge, whose mind was like a many lettered encyclopaedia, we see what stores of learning and conversation may be accumulated by memory. In men again like Sir Walter Scott, who never saw a place without seeming to retain a photographic impression of it, we notice how this faculty can, as it were, hang round pleasant pictures in the mind; and in the case of individuals like Louis Philippe, who could remember faces not seen for many years, we may learn how much a good memory bears on the successful management of life. It is not given to many to have memories such as these persons had; but by moderate care and cultivation memory may become to all a well-ordered storehouse of agreeable facts and impressions reproducible at will."[1]

A few years ago I met the great "memory man" —Datas—at the Palace Theatre, London. I have always had the greatest admiration for his wonderful mnemonic powers and I was anxious to learn something of his *modus operandi*; but was a little diffident in approaching the subject. Unfortunately " Datas " had heard some of my " impressions " and would talk of nothing but mimicry, and before I could get on to the subject of memory I was called away.

Fortunately " Datas " has written a book, in which he has given an outline of his wonderful " memory training." The book is called *Memory*, by " Datas," and is published by Messrs. Gale and Polden, 2 Amen Corner, Paternoster Row, E.C.

" Datas " insists on cultivating the faculties of observation and concentration. This appears to be the secret of the whole system of Memory training, as it is certainly the secret of the Art of Mimicry.

" The first rule to put in practice," says Datas,

---

[1] W. Haigh Miller: *The Culture of Pleasure.*

" is to concentrate your thought wholly upon that which you are anxious to remember, and to apply such concentration of thought to one thing at a time. No other subject must intrude, your undivided attention must be given in one direction only. Nor is this alone sufficient. You must apply yourself in the most diligent manner of which you are capable to your subject, so that the knowledge you gain of it is a lasting one and of such strength that it sets up an impression in your mind which can never be effaced. ' The law of association ' is one most helpful to all ' memory students '—in fact one may almost go so far as to say that it is practically the one real ' help,' regarded as a help, pure and simple. One idea begets another, therefore, when memorizing one idea, kill two birds with one stone, and also memorize the corresponding idea. Nor are you necessarily confined to the two. Sometimes you will find that a whole string of ideas cluster around one—a veritable parent idea, and in such cases you must memorize all. It may be that you will not at once discover the associated idea or ideas. Here you will again perceive the necessity for a searching analysis of your subject matter. You must go over it again and again and endeavour to obtain every associated idea in connection with each idea it gives you.

"For example, suppose you wish to remember the date of the opening of the first railway line in England, there the dominant idea is that of railways. If you have read a great deal about railways, you begin to run through in your mind various facts dealing with them. Incidentally the figure of George Stephenson arises before you ; you recall the date of his birth, etc., the year of the great financial railway bubble, the opening of the Mont Cenis and Simplon Tunnels, the attempts (with eventual success) to tunnel under the Thames, and, of course, Isambard Brunel, the dates of notable collisions, etc. ; a host of things come to mind, the mine of recollection fired by the magic word ' railways.' Time-dates can be readily associated. Take the year 1903. A notable event during that year was Mr. Chamberlain's announcement of his new fiscal policy. We will take it for granted that we remember that. Now in remembering it, just run over other notable events which occurred in the same year—the death of the Pope—the abnormal rainfall—the Dougal and Hickman tragedies, the sale of the *Encyclopædia Britannica* at half price—etc., associate them and impress them on your mind, taking care to also note the day of the month where given, and at any future time when asked for the year of the record rainfall for the British Isles, you will be able to as readily proffer information on the Papal Encyclical or the *Times* bargain !

" Another excellent manner in which dates may be associated is to take a certain date and reckon so many years before or after it—from one year to six thousand. Say you have the Great Fire of London, 1666. Go back to 1066—the year William the Conqueror landed at Pevensey and commenced the conquest of England.

" Where you have ideas which are, so to speak, unconnected it is essential that, in order to commit them to memory successfully, you should establish an intermediary idea as a connecting link. . . . Sir Isaac Newton discovered the law of gravitation by watching an apple fall from a tree on the ground. You wish to remember Newton—gravitation, the link is the word apple. You will say to yourself an apple falls to the ground, falling is in itself an act of gravitation. Who watched a similar action and noted the result ?—Newton. Curiously enough, in this case, you have an extra aid by reason of a certain sort of apple being named the ' Newton ' pippin after the great scientist.

" Often contrast steps in to one's aid, also. Dante's *Inferno* reminds you of Milton's *Paradise Lost*— General ' Tom Thumb ' calls to mind the ' Polish Giant ' and the ugliness of Wilkes gives rise to thoughts of the beauty of the Duchess of Gainsborough.

" You must take one thing at a time, give it your closest attention and gain the clearest mental impression of it that you can. Assimilate its knowledge, connect its ideas with ideas of a similar character, or link them with ideas nearly similar. Note resemblance with any other ideas ; if possible endeavour to strike a contrast, then store away such knowledge you have acquired ready for future use, and above all things, train yourself in the ready use of it.   Live a careful life, study when in your most vigorous mood, never overdo things, and you will never lack results." [1]

The intelligent reader will read, mark, learn and make the most of this " Datas " system and endeavour to put his theories into practice.   He gives some very valuable suggestions but he is careful not to reveal too much.   He is, no doubt, to a certain extent pledged to secrecy.

The basis of the whole system of memory training is the power of concentration and association of ideas.

" The habit may be cultivated in an adult, but observation may be made a child's second nature if his parents would only take the trouble to cross-question him on everything he sees and hears— the sermon at church ; the public speech ; the school lecture ; the change of the seasons ; the exigencies of agriculture ; and a thousand other subjects affording facilities for observation ; and the very fact of being questioned about them serves to impress them indelibly on the mind." [2]

In order to grasp any subject quickly and thoroughly, don't dwell on isolated details and examples, but mark out the fundamental principles.   Get a good mental grasp of the whole scheme, and gradually assimilate the salient points.   Bring your mind

[1] Datas : *Memory.*
[2] E. O. Bleackley : *Effective Reading.*

to bear on these and then go through the whole work more thoroughly, noticing the properties and accidents of the various propositions.

In these days of mania for collecting old furniture and art treasures, it is fitting and profitable to choose a favourite subject and gradually accumulate everything that has any bearing on it. Surround yourself with appropriate books and pictures. Associate with people who are experts in the matter. Let us suppose you wish to write an essay on the *Morality of the [Drama.* You must try to look at the question dispassionately. Mrs. Grundy is ever ready and willing to supply you with information. It may not be original, but there it is—precise, proper and second-hand ; but then, get her point of view ; you need not agree with it.

Next visit an old actor of experience. Actors are not as difficult to meet as the uninitiated sometimes imagine. Get the entrée into a bohemian club and let yourself go a bit. When you meet the great personality, stand him a drink at once ; don't forget this. He may refuse—at first. But, no doubt, you will gain your ends in time, and will leave with some valuable information and an excellent biography. I am afraid at the first interview the great man will not be inclined to talk about many great exponents of the drama. He will confine himself to his own point of view ; occasionally pausing, Macready like, for effect—and to raise his glass ! Listen to the oracle :—" The others, by——(invoking his Patron Saint) were like nothing on——earth, but—wait and see—*my* performance, laddie, at the Star Theatre on Monday fortnight. I've ' let it rip ' before, and by——(quoting his Patron) I'll ' let it rip ' again ! By George ! Yes, thank you, I will have another ! Here's luck ! "

For such an important essay you will require to know something of the elements of psychology. Call on a Jesuit Priest. He will be delighted to see you. Any difficulties you may have he will immediately clear away. He will anticipate your very thoughts, and give you some very clear practical information in a nutshell.

What has all this to do with memory ? A very great deal. It is a system. You have chosen a subject. You have surrounded yourself with appropriate books, pictures and people. You are gradually training your senses. You are creating an atmosphere. Everything has tended to foster your faculties of observation, concentration and comparison. By the time your essay is finished such an impression has been made on your mind as will not readily be effaced.

In the same way establish a system in developing the Art of Mimicry. Let your surroundings be utilized to foster your resources. Make the world and human nature your incessant study on the lines that I have indicated.

For the purposes of the drama a special memory is requisite. Both Sir Herbert Tree and Mr. Harry

Fragson have these special talents. (They are excellent subjects for mimicry. I recommend you to immediately study them and include them in your repertoire. Sir Herbert as " Billy Brown of London " and Mr. Harry Fragson as Hamlet would be funny !)

What is this special memory ? What is the drama ? The drama is action. Acting is a combination of vocal intonation, gesture, facial expression, movement. They are all associated and form part of one homogeneous whole. A part can only be memorized then during rehearsal. The tone of the voice, as well as the action and spoken line, suggests the cue. Acting is not an independent art like mimicry. All the characters of the play must work together, and they are all dependent on each other. Amateurs don't realize this when they fail to turn up at rehearsal. They never seem to be aware that all concerned in the play suffer by their absence.

If you would like to indulge in a splendid exercise for your nerves and temper, produce a piece at your own expense at a London theatre and engage both amateurs and professionals to take part in it. When the affair is over, you will not be anxious to indulge in a similar experiment. You will consider that more than enough is worse than a feast ; and so, no doubt, will your friends and relations who have been present at the performance and have formed a lower estimate of your talents and foresight. The press, whose business it is to be present, will bless

E

you and will signify their approval by their kindly notices of your beautiful play, which, by the way— unlike those manuscripts of their own, in their dusty pigeon-holes—is produced, has lived and died. *Requiescat in pace.*

If your efforts at mimicry are not successful you might try your hand at writing a play. They are both interesting pursuits. The basis of both is a knowledge of the stage. In both arts you must analyse methods, situations, types, characters, everything. You must learn to think logically; study motives, classification, sequence, analogy. In both arts you must learn to feel, study nature, and possess a keen sense of humour.

The study of logic is the basis of every creative art or science. If more people studied it, there would be fewer failures.

How many people can define? How many people are quick to grasp incongruous analogies, or subtle analysis. But, if you wish to be a successful mimic, you must train your mind to perceive, and work quickly and accurately. You must cultivate your sensory and motor memory, sense perception, nervous force, the dramatic and humorous faculties, and the vocal organs. Acquire pliability, strength of will and great powers of reproduction and retention, and I hope you will feel all the better for it!

A bad memory is, no doubt, a defect, but then some of the cleverest men have had bad memories;

perhaps because their heads are so crowded with ideas that they chase one another round the brain, and form an inconsequential chaos.

Want of system, a partiality for the bottle, and general debauchery are, no doubt, in some cases responsible. Nature abhors inconsequence; and, if a wretched individual's good qualities are disconnected and inconsequential, she arbitrarily steps in and forces him to be systematic—in the wrong way! Perhaps that is the reason that human frailty and genius are so often allied.

Read *Memory and its Cultivation* by Edridge-Green, and write to Messrs. Pelman-Foster for their system of Memory training. They have the secret of securing certainty in recollection and an excellent method, which I cannot too highly recommend. Their address is, 4 Bloomsbury St., W.C. You will never regret a course of lessons which will enable you to remember details easily, and get in the habit of comparing, classifying, defining and using your reasoning faculties. It provides valuable and interesting exercises for the proper use of the senses. It will enable you to pay closer attention to everything, to think logically and accurately without any effort.

CHAPTER VI

The Imagination

IMAGINATION is a faculty of the mind by which it conceives and forms ideas of things communicated to it by the organs of sense.

" Imagination," says Bacon, " I understand to be the representation of individual thought."

According to Granville, " Simple apprehension of corporeal objects, if present, is sense, if absent is imagination."

" Imagination," says Father Maher, " may be defined as the faculty of forming mental images or representations of material objects, apart from the presence of the latter. The representation so formed is called in nearly all recent psychological literature an *idea*."

The stronger your imagination, the more original will be your powers of mimicry.

" If I mistake not, the ' creative instinct ' exists in all men to some extent—feeble in some, perceptible in others, brilliant in the great inventors." [1]

A rich and fertile imagination is a great gift which,

---

[1] Ribot : *Creative Imagination.*

used with discretion, is of incalculable benefit to the artiste. W. Haigh Miller says : " The imagination is a faculty which largely ministers to the. enjoyment of life, as it is prudently or imprudently exercised. Some men are sadly deficient in this power. In the fairest landscape they will, as was remarked of an eminent barrister, pull out a dry law-paper, and read it with gusto, instead of looking around them with ecstasy. At the seaside, amidst setting suns, tawny sands and purple seas, they will think, like the subject of one of John Leech's caricatures, chiefly of shrimps for breakfast.

" To the imagination we owe the enjoyment that is reaped from the poet's labours, from Homer and Shakespeare down to the fugitive verses in the corner of the newspaper. To this faculty are due all the pleasures of fiction—a pleasure undoubtedly most keen, although too often deplorably abused.

" An over-active imagination, however, becomes a dreadful tormentor, and requires careful restraint, if it would not lead its owner to the borders of in-sanity. The hypochondriac, under its influence, succumbs to all sorts of diseased fancies. The poor student imagined that he had swallowed a cobbler ; a philosopher fancied that he was changed into a grain of wheat, and was afraid to walk about lest he should be picked up by a fowl ; another, in all his walks, saw a grisly skeleton accompanying him. The undue cultivation of the imagination leads also to great waste of mental power. The habitual devourer of novels can seldom bear wholesome intellectual food. The late Sir James Mackintosh lost much of his valuable time in day dreams. He led two distinct lives, we are told. In one, he was himself, the worthy Scottish Baronet, in the other, giving reins to his imagination, he was an Eastern Emperor, ruling over millions of men, leading armies, and making conquests. Coleridge, the poet, led also a dreaming life, under the influence of an unregulated imagination, projecting too many works that went little further than the mere conception of them. Many men of less note than he, too, have equally allowed their imagination to run riot—life under its influence being a work always about to be begun, but never beginning to any good purpose." [1]

If you have been putting into practice the hints I have given in the chapter on " First Principles," and have exercised your senses daily, you will have been fostering your imaginative powers, be they great or small, though you knew it not. Your brain will have become more fertile in ideas : the exercise of your senses will have produced an alertness and originality in your perception of things ; your will has been strengthened ; there is a power and individuality that was entirely absent before. Already the mind is being trained, with more or less facility, to conjure up fantasies, imageries, and conceptions ; it is becoming stronger and healthier.

[1] W. Haigh Miller : *The Culture of Pleasure.*

You have learned to elaborate and evolve situations, and symbols, from the slightest materials. First comes the idea, the slender outline of impressions, which gradually takes form and vividness, possessing characteristic properties and accidents ; lastly original local colouring, and " little touches " of invention are added. The impression becomes creative and individual—the very antithesis of reproduction or servile copy. You have no wish to degenerate into a parrot, mocking bird, or mere buffoon. Then stimulate this subtle imaginative faculty, if you wish to develop into a great artist.

" When we speak of an imaginative person, we usually mean a person who does not merely visualize clearly, but one who combines his images in new ways, not in strict accordance with actual fact. . . . Some habitually retain and revive visual images ; others auditory ones, that is images, of sound ; others motor ones, that is, images of movement ; others tactile, that is, images derived from touch. . . . Our history and experience, our education, our emotional condition, our natural temperament, our race and religion, all predispose us in various ways. We never get free from the predisposition. . . . If a student of religious ceremonies is taken into a church during Mass he absolutely sees different sights from a man who cares for none of these things." [1]

When visiting a great city, notice every place of

[1] F. Ryland : *The Story of Thought and Feeling.*

interest in it. When going over an old castle find out its history and all the legends concerning it. Compare it with the manners and customs of the present day—noticing the effect of the advancement of learning, civilization, and development of manners and habits.

When you enter the ancient cathedral, notice the style of its architecture, the various tombs, the piscina, the different chapels, the old candlesticks. This should lead to a comparison between the ancient and the more modern forms of worship and ritual. Try to discover their agreements and differences. Analyse these and arrive at their first principles and the results of each. This may lead to a deduction of the effects of reformations and revolutions, of destruction and construction. Another thought may strike you—the advantages of unity? From a meditation on the subject of unity you may be led to a meditation on truth, and then to the discovery that truth and unity are convertible terms.

It was the strong imagination of the Greeks that inspired their drama. To them "every River, Mountain or Forest had not only its own special Deity, but in some sense was itself instinct with life. They were not only peopled by nymphs and fauns, were not only the favourite abodes of Water, Forest, or Mountain spirits, but they had a conscious existence of their own." [1]

[1] Sir John Lubbock: *The Beauties of Nature.*

Temperament, that we hear so much about, nowadays, is nothing but the cultivation of the imagination.

The majority of critics, if asked to define the difference between the great artiste and his inferior brother, would no doubt at once say, the one possesses temperament and personal magnetism, while the other has not these qualifications. The one is a creator, the other a reproducer. The general public are not expected to notice these fine points. At one time Mr. Albert Chevalier and Mr. Gus Elen were placed on an equality. Some people would see no difference between a Dan Leno and a Herbert Campbell. To them they would simply be two comedians. An original, humorous mimic and a parrot they would place on the same footing. The truculent Club bore, and a Samuel Foote would be to them both equally diverting. Some people are quite unable to grasp fine points. They have no powers of discrimination.

If you wish to be a great artiste, you must learn to find subtle differences, you must develop a temperament, a magnetism, an imagination. Can they be acquired? I wonder! I cannot undertake the responsibility of answering that question.

Go into coteries where talent and originality prevail. Go into Bohemia; there you will find imagination and ability; but in Society, the social club, the Park, you may look for it in vain. There the majority are fashioned in one mediocre plane of British conventionality.

If you have naturally a strong imagination, and are developing it more and more in the study of mimicry, let me give you a word of warning. Don't dwell too much on the heights, but come to earth now and then ! Don't be too technical ; the general public will not understand you. Your great desire and object must be to please and play up to your various audiences. Try to adapt yourself to various coteries. The more artistic and idealistic your work, the less it will be appreciated by the ordinary members of society. Artistes will appreciate you, but you wish to appeal to a wider class ; besides artistes are not always too charitable. Therefore, discriminate and adapt yourself to your surroundings, and try to present a repertoire of " impressions " that will appeal to all.

The more you bring your imaginative qualities to bear upon your impressions, the further removed will you be from the " phonographic convention," as Mr. Max Beerbohm expresses it. His canons of the art, at the beginning of my introduction, are excellent, and I advise you to work on the lines that he has laid down.

Imagination is an indispensable quality for mimicry at its best. All great mimics have possessed it to a remarkable degree. They have portrayed the very thoughts and characteristics of their subjects under the most incongruous situations.

Sir W. Hamilton has classified the various faculties requisite for the growth of the intellect and imagination.

1. The *Presentative* faculty, i.e. the power of recognizing the various aspects of the world without and the mind within, called in the one case *external perception* and in the other *perception*.

2. The *Conservative* faculty, i.e. the power of storing up impressions to be afterwards reproduced as occasion requires.

3. The *Reproductive* faculty or the means of calling up the dormant impressions into consciousness again.

4. The *Representative* faculty, which determines the greater or less vividness of the impressions or ideas thus produced.

5. The *Elaborative* faculty, or the powers of comparison.

Don't despair if you do not succeed, at first, in reaching an ideal state of perfection. Don't attempt too much. Work on a gradual system, such as I have suggested, and eventually your powers of imagination will increase. " Nothing is denied to well directed industry." Study then the best models assiduously, and practise continually. Read the lives of great actors and entertainers. As your powers of observation and perception develop, so will your imagination.

Don't be afraid to exaggerate freely and to lay on your effects with a bold hand. Build up your creations gradually, magnifying all your subject's little mannerisms and tricks of " voice, speech, and gesture."

Never forget the fable of the " Lion and the Man." It is possible to be witty without being personal.

CHAPTER VII

Voice, Speech, and Gesture

IT is necessary to study the art of Elocution.
There is a standard book published by Messrs.
C. W. Deacon & Co., entitled *Voice, Speech, and
Gesture.* It contains most practical instructions,
and a splendid collection of many selections from
works of modern and Elizabethan writers. The
volume was dedicated to the late Clifford Harrison
and contains numerous recitals from his delightful
repertoire. There is no better book published.
Arm yourself with it at once, and join a good dramatic
club and determine to study the art of acting and
reciting.

" Power is with the tongue : power is with those
who can speak," said Lord Salisbury.

Study under some qualified professor. Go to a
leading actor from choice, a man of good repute and
character, or some entertainer who has made his name
in London and the provinces. " All time and money
spent in training the voice and the body," said Mr.
Gladstone, " is an investment that pays a larger
interest than any other." It is important to train

them both—in the right way. There are a great many quacks which I urge you to avoid. Go to some one of intelligence and distinction, although his terms may be high. You will find it far cheaper in the end. What is the good of going to some self-styled musical professor whom the public cannot stand at any price ; who has been weighed in the balance and found wanting ?

" I think," Mr. Ruskin said, " that general public feeling is tending to the admission that accomplished education must include not only full command of expression by language, but command of true musical sound by the voice."

" Elocution forms a main ingredient in the art of acting." [1]

The art of the actor according to Macready is " To fathom the depths of character, to trace its latent motives, to feel its finest quiverings of emotion, to comprehend the thoughts that are hidden under words and thus possess oneself of the individual man."

" A great actor," Mr. Hermann Vezin once told me, " should be a great teacher. The public don't want anything, they take what is given to them, and are thankful when it is good."

They are often disappointed. Poor public, dear, long-suffering public ! It is the exponents of the drama that require reforming, not popular taste.

---

[1] *Voice, Speech and Gesture.*

You cannot expect the average actor to realize this ; he is, as a rule, far too conceited.

" The actor's business," said the late Sir Henry Irving, " is primarily to reproduce the ideas of the author's brain, to give them form and substance, colour and life, so that those who behold the action of a play may, so far as this can be effected, be lured into the fleeting belief that they behold reality."

If you are in earnest and wish to succeed, go on the stage, if possible. Learn all about " flats," " flies," " floats," " front cloths " and " back cloths," " half sets," and " full sets," and all the positions, entrances and openings of the stage.

Should you be cast for the same part as some leading actor, whom you have seen, don't imitate his methods. This is fatal, except in the case of burlesques.

An amateur friend of mine, some time ago, was excellent the first night of a certain play we produced. He was easy and natural, but the second night his performance had undergone a strange and terrible deterioration. At the end of the play he asked me what I thought of him. " What on earth has happened to you ? " I replied. " You were quite different last night." " Oh," he said, " I have been imitating Charles Wyndham the whole evening."

Study the history of the stage. Observe and reflect as you read. See " reflected the most piquant conditions of life, emotions, humours as in a mirror, with all that interests our curiosity and passions. . . . This feeling has come to us from the days of the great actors and the great plays . . . from the time when the fine actor or actress was as conspicuous a personage as a prime minister, and the night of his finest impersonation as important as that of a great bill or debate." [1]

Get Dr. Doran's *Annals of the English Stage ; Romance of the English Stage, Life of David Garrick,* and *Samuel Foote* by Percy Fitzgerald ; *The London Stage,* by Barton Baker ; *Actors of the Century,* by Frederic Whyte.

Strive to be an original thinker, a creative artiste, and not a mere imitator. You cannot do better than study Nature, and the elements of psychology. You will find Granger's *Psychology* a useful book. After reading that you might get Father Maher's exhaustive and learned treatise. You will find a study of the " Science of Mind " an invaluable basis for your art. Speech was not given us " to conceal our thoughts." It is the expression of the mind. Remember that " labour is the purchase price of success." The study of books should never supersede the study of Nature.

Polygnotus painted his celebrated " Triumph of Miltiades " by public desire, and the Athenian Council proclaimed that he should be maintained at the public expense wherever he went. He received the homage of the whole nation. How different from

[1] Percy Fitzgerald : *Romance of the English Stage.*

the modern English spirit which is inclined to disparage and under-estimate art and artistes !

My uncle, the late E. O. Bleackley, wrote a very interesting essay on *Effective Reading*. It is so full of valuable information that I cannot do better than quote a few passages from it :

" A moment's reflection will convince any man that the most wonderful art, and the basis of all knowledge, lies in the faculty of reading; a power that only excites astonishment when it is found a man does not possess it. . . . A knowledge of elocution enhances the value of all education and may transform the driest subject into one of brilliant attractiveness.

" I do not propose to wade through the rules of elocution as to the mode of dealing with articulation, pronunciation, modulation, accent, emphasis, pause inflection, gesture, etc. ; on these matters I refer you to the successor of Sheridan, the undoubted father of English Elocution, Mr. Walker, from whom all subsequent writers on this subject pilfer their rules, and adopt not only his virtues, but his errors. Walker invented a system out of chaos, framed rules to classify and organise a science, hitherto without basis or guide.   One of his recent imitators —after carefully re-writing his principal rules, had by way of a change, two pages of gasping caverns engraved, supposed to represent the human mouth in the various throes of articulation, ejecting vowels and consonants.   To my mind, they looked more like

F

a score of whistling oysters. He next adopted the advice of Demosthenes as a motto for the title page, and called it " Action," evidently unaware that *actio* with the Romans means the general delivery, and that Demosthenes, when asked the first, second, and third points of eloquence, replied " Delivery," not action. Delivery includes everything] connected with the utterance of speech—the modulation of the voice,┊gesture, etc. However, as this professor of ₍elocution had the good sense to dedicate ┊his work to. a live bishop, it passed muster amongst the other tons of spoilt paper.

" One vocal example of forcible pronunciation is worth a volume of explanatory rule as to how it ought to be done. Study graceful orators, great actors, and the acquisition of elocutionary knowledge at once becomes the most agreeable of sciences.

" It may be said that one of the great secrets of the art of reading is simplicity, an entire absence of the desire to make a point where none could possibly exist, a calm and natural mode of saying a commonplace thing in a commonplace manner ; not, however, indifferent to the excitement of passion, the pathos of love, or the dignity of command ; avoiding, on the one hand, the tiring monotony of the schoolboy, and on the other eschewing the inflated pomposity of the would-be tragedian. Identify yourself with the language you may be uttering, *feel* what you say ; if you entreat, adopt the trembling notes of supplication ; if you command use the dignified, deep-toned calmness of conscious power. Do not stoop into your chest, as if you were ashamed of what you are uttering, but keep your head upright, like a man, and above all, remember Mrs. Siddons' first direction to her pupils, ' Take Time.'

" I remember the late Mr. Vandenhoff giving a clerical elocutionary entertainment in the then well-hole lecture room of the Athenaeum. The place was crowded with clergymen, and the way Vandenhoff read the first chapter of Genesis rather astonished those who up to that time had only regarded it as a somewhat dry record of the creation of the world.

" It is very singular that amongst so large a body of educated men so few seem to be at all impressed with the grand language they are called upon to utter, or endeavour to pronounce it with solemnity and dignity. They gabble through the mandates of the Deity like a schoolboy reading a paragraph from a newspaper, and rattle off the Lord's Prayer as if it were a command instead of an intercession. They ramble through our beautiful liturgy in tones of declamation instead of supplication, leaving little or no good impression behind, reading all that comes in their way with an indifferent air, and a monotonous mediocrity of expression.

" One of the chief advantages to be derived from the study of elocution is a taste for reading which it creates ; a thirst for knowledge which, like the green-

eyed monster, doth make the meat it feeds on.   It
incites a love of language, a natural improvement in
the power of expression ; and can there be anything
more agreeable, more endearing, more profitable,
or more refining, than elegant language ?   The low
price at which the classical productions of our best
authors are now offered, the easy access to our public
libraries and the advantages of a cheap daily press,
afford, nowadays, no excuse for absolute ignorance—
that wonderful and accessible press which has done
more to refine and educate the people during the
present century than all the books published for
the last two hundred years ;   the press, which by
the magic of its genius, translates a dry, ineffective,
and inartistic speech into a brilliant oration and
presents you with a prompt, well considered and
gracefully written leader on interesting topics of
latest occurrence ;   that press which in a quarter of a
century has altogether reformed the old fashioned
and incomprehensible punctuation of fossilized
authors, and introduced an understandable system of
high pointing by the more frequent use of the comma,
banishing the colon and substituting the dash.

" From   the   greatly   increasing   circulation   of
literature generally it is safe to infer that a taste
for reading has been implanted, and is gradually
developing itself, and the mind of this great country
becoming every day more assimilated.

" It is far better to read only light, frivolous
literature than none at all, but the advantage of a

well selected library is incalculable. Perhaps the most profitable plan is to follow a course of directed reading for the attainment of a particular object.

" I was present at the Manchester Mechanics' Institute when Macready was tempted to emerge from his retirement in order to benefit that excellent institution, and never shall I forget the intellectual treat of that evening. The place was crammed by a breathlessly attentive audience, and for two hours that grand tragedian held us all spellbound. His rendering of Pope's ' Dying Christian ' was almost supernatural, and had a wonderfully electrical effect. The reading over, an enthusiastic vote of thanks was carried by acclamation, and he replied by reciting Leigh Hunt's apologue ' Abou Ben Adhem ' and those were the last tones I heard from that wonderfully gifted man. In his introduction Macready beautifully said :—' We are often made sensible of particular habits of thought and language by hearing them from another voice, when they would fail to affect and impress themselves on our minds by the page beneath our eyes.' " [1]

The more you study and strive to make yourself master of the dramatic art, the better able will you be to burlesque it.

Choose effective dramatic recitals. I strongly recommend " At the Opera," " A Charming Woman," " The Story of the Monk Felix," " The Bishop and the Caterpillar," " Dat First Soot," " Yawcob

[1] E. O. Bleackley : *Effective Reading.*

Strauss" and the " Raven "—this is the most difficult
and effective piece in the repertoire of a finished
reciter, but don't mimic the Raven like some mis-
guided amateurs I have heard ! This piece may
be hackneyed. Scores of people recite it, I know—
but how ? " Retrospection " is also a most dramatic
piece. Two of my favourite recitals are " King
Robert of Sicily " and " King John and the Abbot."
Two excellent comedy sketches are " Tantler's
Sister " and the " Lancet."

When you have learnt to produce your voice ;
to speak effectively with appropriate modulation and
gesture ; when you have acquired dramatic knowledge and instinct, you can proceed to practise the
Art of Mimicry.

CHAPTER VIII

Success or Failure ?

"FAILURE and Success, passed away from Earth, and found themselves in a Foreign Land. Success still wore her laurel-wreath which she had won on Earth. There was a look of ease about her whole appearance ; and there was a smile of pleasure and satisfaction on her face, as though she knew she had done well, and had deserved her honours.

"Failure's head was bowed : no laurel-wreath encircled it. Her face was wan, and pain-engraven. She had once been beautiful, and hopeful, but she had long since lost both hope, and beauty. They stood together, these two, waiting for an audience with the Sovereign of the Foreign Land. An old grey-haired man came to them and asked their names.

" ' I am Success,' said Success, advancing a step forward, and smiling at him, and pointing to her laurel-wreath.

" He shook his head.

" ' Ah,' he said, ' do not be too confident. Very often things go by opposites in this land. What you call Success we often call Failure ; what you call Failure, we call Success. . . . Those flowers yonder : for us they have a fragrant charm ; we love to see them near us. But you do not even take the trouble to pluck them from the hedges where they grow in rich profusion. So, you see, what we value as a treasure you do not value at all.'

" Then he turned to Failure. ' And your name ? ' he asked kindly, though indeed he must have known it.

" ' I am Failure,' she said sadly.

" He took her by the hand.

" ' Come now, Success,' he said to her, ' let me lead you into the Presence Chamber.'

" Then she who had been called Failure, and was now called Success, lifted up her bowed head and raised her weary frame, and smiled at the music of her new name. And with that smile she regained her beauty, and her hope. And hope having come back to her, all her strength returned.

" ' But what of her ? ' she asked regretfully of the old grey-haired man ; ' must she be left ? '

" ' She will learn,' the old man whispered, ' she is learning already. Come now, we must not linger.'

" So she of the new name passed into the Presence Chamber. But the Sovereign said :—

" ' The world needs you, dear and honoured worker. You know your real name : do not heed what the world may call you. Go back, and work, but take with you this time unconquerable hope.'

" So she went back, and worked, taking with her unconquerable hope, and the sweet remembrance of the Sovereign's words and the gracious music of her Real Name."[1]

Success or Failure depends entirely upon our ideals. " High failure overleaps the bound of low successes." Don't be disappointed if you don't come up to your expectations. " There is many a slip 'twixt the cup and the lip," and your defeat may not be your fault. If you have honestly striven to perfect yourself in your art ; if you have had a high ideal ; if you have tried to elevate, to evoke mirth and laughter, to cheer many sadly in want of brightness, to create peace and harmony in a " vale of tears," you have not laboured in vain. What has been your aim and intention ? Was it to gain renown ; to make money ; to carry all before you ; to hold up some *bête noire* to ridicule, hatred, or contempt ; or to develop your talents ; to provide healthy amusement ; to elevate your neighbour and yourself ?

If you labour long and earnestly you are bound to succeed.

" To go about whining, and bemoaning your pitiful lot because we fail in achieving that success in life, which after all depends rather upon habits of industry, and attention to business details than upon knowledge, is the mark of a small, and often

[1] Beatrice Harraden : *Failure and Success.*

of a sour mind. . . . Benjamin Constant, with his splendid talents, contrived to do nothing ; and after living for many years miserable, he died worn out and wretched. . . . Coleridge, in many respects, resembled Constant. He possessed equally brilliant powers, but was similarly infirm of purpose. . . . There is, perhaps, no station in life in which difficulties have not to be encountered, and overcome before any decided measure of success can be achieved. Those difficulties are, however, our best instructors, as our mistakes often form our best experience." [1]

This life is a battle, we live in a selfish world. You will encounter scores of people in your career, for ever striving to get the better of you, to hound you out of your life ; to fawn and extol you before your face, and deride you behind your back. It is necessary to be always on your guard. The great Homer sometimes nodded. If you are engaged in business, you must cultivate business instincts. Take every one's measure. Be polite to all. You can do this, and, at the same time, not be a prig. Priggishness and snobbishness are signs of mental limitation. Snobs are always very well pleased with themselves on the principle that " ignorance is bliss."

I was discussing a well-known bohemian the other day with a very gifted artiste, and he said—mentioning the individual in question—" He will never advance any further. What he is now, he will always

[1] Samuel Smiles : *Self Help*.

be." " What else could he desire ? " I replied,
" he has an excellent opinion of himself." " Ah,
that's the trouble ! " said my friend. How trenchant
and how true ! What a warning to us. If we wish
to advance in our various vocations we must be
for ever humble.

If you are endowed with a powerful imagination,
and a faculty for imitation, be careful to study only
the best models ; otherwise these very virtues will
turn against you, and be your downfall. They
are powerful gifts—used in the right way. There
is nothing more dangerous than a perversion of
natural talents. The greatest men, when they fail,
fall the most deeply, because they are so near the
light. The corruption of the best is always the
worst. Disease attacks the healthiest bodies the
most severely. Your great talents should make
you very humble.

Don't be a mere imitator. Strive to be a creative
artiste. Think, observe, create a system, labour
incessantly, and " look at Nature, and see how it
affects your mind."

Bring your mind to bear upon the smallest
details. Remember the first principles and basis
of all art is concentration and observation.

Perceive and analyse everything. Should you
fail, you must console yourself with the fact that
you have persevered ; that you have worked on a
true method ; that failure is only relative. It may
have been owing to the fact of uncongenial sur-

roundings ; or the lack of a word of encouragement or sympathy at the right moment.

The essence and fundamental principle of all art is the power of analysis. People will not analyse. " Know thyself "—that wonderful Greek adage—is written in heaven. It is too high an ideal for most of us. It was inscribed in gold letters over the portico of the temple at Delphi. It is only in our best moments that we nearly reach this high standard of perfection. For the most part we dwell in a groove. We are too inclined to pander to Mrs. Grundy. She is immensely proper, and wise—a creature to be feared, and imitated. Oh, wonderful ideal ! How glorious is conventional propriety, but how disastrous to original thought, and creative art !

A young actor of ability with too much money, and influence, and lacking the right counsel and warning at the right moment, goes from bad to worse. His methods degenerate into mannerisms, his style becomes stilted, and finally, he becomes stone blind to his own limitations, and all for want of observation and introspection. He has never " known himself." Bad habits grow. We wake up sometimes to discover the tyranny of talents misdirected. Custom has conquered ; the network of association has gathered round us, holding us in its iron meshes ; it has stifled our senses, and will— while all the time we have been asleep ! The brain is composed of innumerable nerve cells, all more or less associated, which affect the whole nervous system. Gradually our reason and will become either stronger or weaker, according to the way in which we have developed our faculties.

Never cease to analyse. Be independent, resourceful, creative. Don't be guided by one personality but use your reason and sense-perception.

The politician that you have admired so much, if the truth was only known, has had his own wretched axe to grind. That amiable divine, whom you have so blindly followed, may not have been in good faith ; that virtue you have so long prided yourself on may be a subtle vice, that self-love has fostered, to which pride has pandered ; and all because you have never analysed.

" Know thyself " and " Be thyself." Be true to your art, and your highest instincts ; and it doesn't very much matter whether the crowd applaud. If you have been true to yourself, and to your conscience, you have been a success.

Vulgar popularity, vulgar sordid aims, the vulgar accumulation of wealth, while your humanity is starving, is failure ; though it may meet with the approbation of the wise fool of a world.

A celebrated artiste with the best possible opinion of himself once urged me to cultivate more confidence ; to come on to the platform, lean leisurely on the piano with extended arms, look defiantly at the audience as much as to say : " Banish your scepticism ! Here I am, you can't get away from

the fact. I am here, you are there. Who are you ?
Look at me ! Now, you've got to listen to me,
whether you like it or not ! "

I was not ungrateful to him for the hint.

I went round to the front, and sat amongst the
audience during his turn. He came on. He was
very fat. He went through his beautiful business.
He lifted up his head, and extended his chest and
his arms. He seemed to be thoroughly enjoying
himself. He was oblivious of the audience, who
looked upon him with awe, and wonder, not unmixed
with scorn, and *sotto voce* sighed, " No origin ! "

What we call success they sometimes pronounce
failure. It all depends upon the true ideal.

Learn to analyse, and to " Know thyself." It
may teach you humility, and save you many a
nerve-destroying shock !

CHAPTER IX

My Method of Working, and Reminiscences

WILHELM KUHE in his *Musical Recollections* says : " But of whatever faults of omission and commission I may be found guilty, I hope, at least, to be acquitted of a charge of thrusting forward my own identity to the exclusion of other and far more interesting personalities in the world of music in which I have spent the greater part of my life. . . . I have sought to forget myself as often as possible."

That, also, has been my aim, and intention, in writing this little treatise. I am anxious though to make it as complete as possible. For the sake of completeness, then, I feel compelled to appear for as short a time as possible upon the stage ; to make my profound bow before a generous public, kindly critics and artistes ; to thank them again and again for the encouraging remarks that they have passed upon my " impressions of leading actors, actresses and vocalists."

On very many occasions I have been asked to explain my method of working. How often have I heard the remarks : " How do you do it ? " " Does it come naturally ? " " Do you practise a great deal ? " " Does it take you long ? " " I don't think you are quite as good as usual," or " You really have improved wonderfully." " Instead of imitations, why not do something original ? I have written a sketch that I think you would do quite nicely." " Have you been long at it ? " " How *do* you change your voice ? " " You change your face too— do you know that ? " " Now, do you think you could imitate *me* ? "

It is very difficult to find the right answers to these numerous questions. Such a lot depends on little accidentals. It would seem that a new impression often comes by chance. It is really the result of frequent visits to the theatres, where one's interest has been greatly aroused. It is impossible to always receive definite impressions and to reproduce at will. One is not always in the same receptive mood. The stress and strain of modern life tend to distract and prevent one from getting just the effect required.

When first I gave an impression of the late Sir Henry Irving many years ago, I imagined him giving a recital of the nursery rhyme " Three Blind Mice," in which I endeavoured to bring out all his mannerisms with wild exaggeration. At the end I staggered and fell into a chair, ejaculating " Rats,

Rats, Rats!" Afterwards when working out impressions of other artistes, I used the same lines as a commencement, and found them a useful basis for reproducing their intonations. When I had gradually caught all their little tricks of voice and gesture, I would work out a little burlesque of their methods, paraphrasing everything.

From my earliest infancy I loved the play-house, with its flavour of orange peel and the solemnity of the green curtain, with the huge lion and unicorn emblazoned upon it. With anxious intensity I sat gazing on the mighty proscenium, eagerly waiting for the commencement of the fairy play. The people who were with me never realized how much I was enjoying myself until I afterwards gave a reproduction of the whole performance. We had a small theatre in our house and regularly enacted plays. I would invariably produce an annual pantomime in a liliputian cardboard theatre every Christmas! At my first school our productions grew more and more frequent. Not only the boys, but all the masters were fired with an enthusiasm for the drama, which superseded the monotonous drudgery of lessons. Gradually the plays were more elaborately mounted. The Head Master and his assistants were busy painting scenery; the Head's wife and the governesses made the costumes. At length our performances were transferred from the schoolroom to the Assembly Rooms, and the Parish Church gained a turret clock.

G

About this time my father took us to London. During the visit we saw Charles Warner in *Drink*, which made the greatest impression upon me. I "took him off" continually. Wherever I went I volunteered to give my latest "impression." My conception grew more and more intense and violent— I frequently broke a few glasses! Gradually this impersonation became less popular, and eventually died a natural death.

What a wonderful actor Charles Warner was! He was simply full of verve and magnetism. In the winter of 1905 at a charity matinée which was given at the Haymarket Theatre, I gave some "impressions." I was very tired, as I had been working very hard at that time, and I felt that my performance commenced very mechanically. Suddenly I was conscious of an intensity and stillness in the theatre that I had seldom experienced. Everything seemed to centre round the O.P. Box—I felt drawn to that Box—I could not help but play to it. I seemed to get effects and tones without the smallest effort. At the conclusion I gave a rapid glance towards that box and recognised Charles Warner.

Afterwards he was very cordial in his praise and asked me if I ever "took him off." I was about to reply in the negative when I suddenly remembered my impersonation of early years.

At Oxford I "took off" various College Dons. The average Don, and especially the Don Divine, has characteristic mannerisms. One hot day towards the close of the summer term, the President of the College wished to see me. My appearance, in cap and gown, in the middle of the afternoon, caused rather a sensation. I rang the bell and asked to see the worthy man.

"He is engaged with all the Dons," the butler said.

"Tell him I've called, please," I replied and withdrew to my "digs" in the town. Presently there was a ring at the front door, and a breathless porter panted out, "The President wishes to see you at once, sir." When I at length arrived at the holy man's rooms on the first floor, I was surprised to find the apartment full of Dons. There was a horrible rustle of silk. (Here my impression commenced with the impersonation of the President's voice and manner, which always produced the greatest hilarity.)

"What the blue-blazes do you mean by it ? Pooh ! Pooh ! Pooh ! Pooh ! Pooh ! You've kept us waiting three-quarters of an hour ! "

The discussion centred round the lecture fee of £7 which I had not paid. Neither had I attended the lectures ; nor had I kept a sufficient number of chapels. They insisted on my paying the lecture fees whether I had attended the lectures or not. They irritated me to such an extent and looked so evil—one of the Dons seemed to me to be coming out in blotches during the interview—that I grew more and more confident in my replies to the

President, who, I felt convinced, was secretly on my side.

"I consider it quite bad enough to be obliged to pay £7 a term lecture fee," I said, "without having the additional infliction of attending them." This "interview with the Dons" never failed to bring down the house.

Both at Oxford and at Repton I went in greatly for reciting and these recitals were tolerated at both places. The friendly criticisms I have received stand out in my memory. Occasionally I have been told that I recalled the methods of Tree, Lewis Waller, Irving, Hermann Vezin, etc., and I was asked if I ever went in for mimicry.

In discussing various plays and players with a friend one evening on the river, we both gave representations of various types and scenes. Shortly after that I was urged to develop the art of mimicry, as it was so popular. I resolved then to try my hand. I practised a little, and found I could catch, more or less, the tones and peculiarities of Irving, Tree, Mrs. Patrick Campbell, Ellen Terry, Wilson Barrett. I added these celebrities to other impersonations of types and gave them with a certain amount of success at various parties.

I visited the theatres and music halls more frequently. I heard the impersonations of Arthur Faber, and Playfair, Farren Soutar and Marie Dainton. I quickly added other well-known people to my repertoire—Lewis Waller, Sir Charles

Wyndham, and Miss Mary [Moore, Martin Harvey, George Alexander, Sir John Hare, Arthur Roberts, Maurice Farkoa, Herbert Campbell, Henry Kemble, Albert Chevalier, Clifford Harrison, Corney Grain, Haydn Coffin. I found these quite enough, and more than enough to go on with, and I have never had to seek for new impressions. Of course, since I started, I have developed a number of new impressions each year, but I have always found people like the old ones best. In fact it is true to say that the old selections are the most popular.

It is always a delight to me to hear a brother mimic. It is a form of entertainment that appeals to me greatly. I have had the pleasure of meeting them all and have always enjoyed their society immensely.

Once, on the South Coast, I met a celebrated and charming lady mimic. We were both appearing at a couple of *al fresco* concerts. Presently she asked me what I was going to do. " I have been asked to do some imitations." " Oh! you wretched man ! " she replied with a smile. I was very gratified to find that this charming lady was one of the loudest in singing my praises afterwards. I remember that one of my chief successes on that day was " Wilson Barrett " and I was greatly congratulated by two of the lady artistes who happened to be in his company. The following day I was very shocked to read of his death.

A well-known mimic at a party a few years ago

said to me "What do you think of this? Our hostess has told me not to do any imitations to-night, as she is expecting some young amateur who goes in for that sort of thing. Who is he, do you know?" It was no good. I had to confess that I was the man! We soon became the greatest friends!

Once at Newquay I was asked to do some "impressions" at their annual Life Boat Demonstration. They had engaged a troupe of Pierrots. One of the members of the troupe commenced to give some imitations. The moment he got to a climax and received a well-merited round of applause, the curtain was lowered upon him! He was righteously indignant, and there was a terrible row, which ended in blows. During the evening the police were called in. It was really the fault of the management. They ought to have made it quite clear there were to be no "imitations." I was particularly upset about it, as I had the greatest regard for this artiste's talent and we were on the friendliest terms. He is one of the finest mimics in England.

My favourite audience is at the Savage Club on Saturday night. I have always found it the most charitable yet critical assembly in London. To do oneself justice there is not always an easy task. I go so far as to say that if you are a success there you will be a success anywhere, and I think most people will agree with me. Savages, and bohemians generally, are loyal and true. They are never tired of their favourite selections, and it is always a pleasure to know this and to gradually gage the Savage taste !

Mimicry is nervous, exacting work. It is sometimes exceedingly tiring and very difficult always to be at concert pitch. People expect one to be always the same, like a bad instrument !

Now my time is up and I must bid farewell. I must quit the heated artificial atmosphere of London for the cool salubrious air of the Surrey hills.

" My very good friends who have liked me ; my very good enemies who have hated me—My dear good women who have not loved me—my poor weak women who have—Emperors, charlatans, pickpockets, good fellows all : here's forgiveness and forgetfulness in this world, and a merry meeting in the next ! Good night ! Good night ! " [1]

[1] Sir Herbert Tree.

CHAPTER X

Some Selections and Suggestions

JUST a few suggestions for working up a repertoire of selections. Beware of giving long recitals. It is important, especially at first, to present a series of snap-shots. Most amateurs make the mistake of wearying the audiences by absurdly long recitations. People will not stand it. Remember that we live in a rapid age, therefore be short, crisp and bright.

The abstracted empyricism of Sir Herbert Tree and the quick vivacity of Mr. Arthur Roberts form a diverting contrast ; therefore you might give an impersonation of them both at rehearsal, after this fashion :—

SIR HERBERT TREE.

I'm afraid I'm a little late, but my cabman didn't know the way. He took me round by Regents Park by mistake. I was going through my lines and he distracted me. Yes, he distracted me through the trap. The silly fellow ! He kept saying,

" Where to sir ? " but that was not my cue. " I
know," I said. " Drive onwards, drive onwards,
drive—drive onwards." He wanted 8s. 6d. but,
the Syndicate must pay. Alfwed—Alfwed—where
is Alfwed ? Ah—Alfwed—bring me a small oyster,
and half a dozen bottles of Pol Roger. Oh ! I mean,
half a dozen oysters from Dwivers, and one small
bottle of Pol Roger !

Where is the " script ? " and a blue pencil ?
Has no one got a blue pencil ? We can't produce the
play without a blue pencil. Ah, thank you ; now we
shall get on. . . . Mr. Arthur Roberts is discovered !

A. Roberts. I thought I was lost.

Tree. No, only a little bit gone in the upper
story—but we can cut it if you like—Where is my
blue pencil ?

A. Roberts. Never mind. This scene is blue
enough—with the gags.

Tree. Couldn't you cut them, Mr. Roberts ?

A. Roberts. I always do—it gives them such
point—Now, for a little quiet study. I'm discovered
O.P. How can I be discovered O.P. ? The author
doesn't know his business. (*Reading*) O.P.—B. and
dash. B. and S. Yes. I'm discovered with a B.
and S. I drink B. and S. and repeat the business
ad lib. It goes down ! (*Sings*)

We'll suppose that you sing a new topical song.
It goes down !
You mention Lloyd George—that the Budget's all wrong.
It goes down !

I think I'll bring down the house with that. B. and S. down C. Fiddle-de-dee ! D.T. Then up a tree ! I beg pardon. It's an interior set !

Tree. Mr. Roberts—will you speak your lines ?

A. Roberts. Speak *my* lines. I always do.

Tree. Yes, but I mean the author's lines. (*Reads*)

A. Roberts. Very pleasant lines. They'll go down well with the business. Now I smash the furniture !

Tree. No—You don't smash the furniture.

A. Roberts. Then —I fall over the mat, and break my neck.

Tree. Oh sun, oh moon, oh stars ! Friends, Romans, Countrymen ! Oh, liquid language of eternity ! Oh ! liquid Pol Roger !

I have many other branches of Tree, who lends himself to mimicry. I have impersonated him in Shakespeare, comedy, tragedy, melodrama, at rehearsal with his wife, when he is not feeling very well, but always with the greatest respect.

Let us now pass on to a general impression of Mr. Martin Harvey—

Mr. Martin Harvey.

Oh ! what a rogue and peasant slave am I !
Is it not monstrous that this player here
That in the " Only Way " and " Cigarette Maker "
Had filled the Theatre
Cannot induce you to frequent the circle
When he produces plays like Hamlet.
It's all for nothing ! For art's not smart.

Poor pigeoned livered British Public
A melodrama's quite the only way for you.

Such as Lucy Manette—a sweet name and a sweet nature. It's not for me, those eyes filled with tears. It's not for me that she is thinking or will ever think! No, no, little Mimi, it's no use. Love is sweet, but liquor's better, and death is best of all!

MISS ELLEN TERRY IN " CAPTAIN BRASSBOUND'S CONVERSION."

Oh, this is a perfectly heavenly place, lovely, lovely, lovely! And the people—the people have such nice faces. Oh, I know they wouldn't hurt me. No. Now, why do people get killed by savages? Why, simply because instead of being nice to them and saying " How do you do ? " like me—why, they aim pistols at them ! Oh, I've been everywhere, I've mixed up with savages and—those people who eat one up—prompter—cannibals. Yes : I've mixed with cannibals, savages, cannibals and savages, and cannibals, and all sorts ! Everybody said they'd kill me, but I simply went up to them and I said : " How do you do ? " and they—they were quite nice.

MR. LEWIS WALLER.

I believe Mr. Waller wants a new play. If Mr. Waller were asked to state his requirements, let us imagine what he would suggest for a *scenario.*

Gentlemen—I am always ready to read a play. Day or night—night or day, and always fair. If you wish to win money write a play like good Monsieur Beaucaire. I must slash about and kill people right, left and centre ! The girl I love cannot love me, because I am a foreigner or have killed some one she doesn't love. Any motive will do that gives me the sympathy of the audience. Then let a lot of people rush on—and off, principally off, and before they have a chance, let me kill them all. Then make the leading lady love me ever so much. Don't forget to give me a recitation in every act, after this fashion :

" Faint with hunger, choking with the dust, dazed from want of sleep, reeling in the saddle until I saw the towers of Nôtre Dame black against the skies of Paris. Was I in time ? The Louvre— the Queen had gone ! Was I too late, too late—My heart beat it, the blood drummed it in my ears. Back from the Louvre here. I staggered up the stairs, and past your watchmen, saw your face. No, not too late. Thank God, I've triumphed. Done your bidding—saved the Queen ! "

SIR CHARLES WYNDHAM AND
MISS MARY MOORE.

Sir Chas. " I've got a motto—always merry and bright,"—bright and merry. Don't look so serious— smile, smile. No ! Popsy-woodle-wee ! Ah ! that's

better. Poor little woman, poor little woman—
Let me try to guide you to the right way——

Miss Moore. The sign-post was so misleading. I
walked, and walked, and walked, and then I saw a
porter. I said to him. " Oh, Mr. Porter, whatever
shall I do ? I wanted to go to Brighton, and here I
am at Kew ! " Just like that. You were speaking
of a new way. You will teach me that new way
dear, won't you ?

Sir Chas. The new way for us is the old way for
the wise. It's a pleasant way, strewn with flowers.
The flowers of self-abnegation. Of sweet reasonable-
ness, of patient tolerance, of earnest trustfulness.
In that way lies peace, the fulfilment of our better
selves, the full golden harvest of love !

Miss Moore. I am not quite sure how much one
ought to be in love—to *be* in love. And yet I feel
that if some strong man strode up to me, and said
" You *shall* ! "—I might. If I only knew the right
way. Sign-posts are so misleading.

Sir Chas. Come to the Carlton ! That's a
pleasant way ? No—ah, it's a pleasant way,
strewn with flowers. You will come ? Ah, dear
little woman, dear little woman, dear little woman !

MRS. PATRICK CAMPBELL.

I went to see Mrs. Patrick Campbell the other
evening. I found her very revolting. I don't

mean disagreeable. Of course, we all know, she is a charming actress, but in the play she was always kicking over the traces. She had a husband, and she defied him. She had a father and mother, and she defied them, and she encouraged her little sister to do the same. They have a scene together something like this :

Ah, my little sister. Our parents want to sell you for money, as they sold me years ago, but they won't succeed. I will prevent it !

I have just told your intended husband exactly what I thought about him. I said " You are ugly, and old, and fat, and my little sister shall never submit to any of your amorous attentions. You dyspeptic looking person ! You callous creature ! "

Oh, my dear, he didn't say much but he looked rather hurt !

My husband hasn't appeared yet and the audience think I've poisoned him. When they find out their mistake ; that I don't kill him, and I don't kill myself—they'll kill the play ! Oh, you little baby, be warned in time, and remember the story of the little girl and the butterflies.

At sixteen years she knew no care.
   Why should she ? sweet and pure as light,
And there pursued her everywhere
   Butterflies all white.

A lover looked, she drooped her eyes
   That glowed like pansies wet with dew,

And lo! there came from out the skies
   Butterflies all blue!

Before she guessed, her heart was gone.
   His tale of love was quickly told!
And all around her wheeled and shone
   Butterflies of gold!

Then he forsook her one sad morn.
   She sobbed and wept—" Oh, love, come back."
There only came to her forlorn
   Butterflies all black!

MISS LENA ASHWELL.

Are you ready for your bicycle
   Loraine, Loraine, Loree—
You're booked to ride your Humber
   To-day at Battersea.
Make no mistake, don't use your brake
   Nor run into a tree!

She clasped her wheezy pug dog,
   Plump Loraine, Loraine, Loree,
I will not ride my Humber
   To-day at Battersea.
It's killed a man, it's killed a boy
   And nearly done for me!

Unless you ride your motor bike
   Loraine, Loraine, Loree,
Unless you ride your motor bike
   For all the crowd to see,

I'll send your wheezy pug dog
    To the home at Battersea !

That husbands can be cruel,
    Quoth Loraine, Loraine, Loree,
That husbands can be cruel
    I have known for seasons three.
That's why I'm rather dull and whine
    As any man can see.

She rode her noisy Humber,
    Oh, a stolid lass was she !
And kept it straight, and won the race
    As near, as near could be.
But she punctured at the bend—the end
    The crowd all laughed to see.
And no one but her wheezy pug
    Was killed at Battersea.

Mr. George Alexander.

Oh, there you are, my dear, there you—now I'm
going to make love to you. Throughout my life
I've made love to all sorts of people—old ladies,
young ladies, housekeepers, girls, queens, after
this fashion :—

" If all my dreams of loveliness had been pieced
together into one perfect woman she would have
been like you. All my life I have read tales of love,
and tried to find their secret in the bright eyes about
me—tried and failed. But when I saw you, the

old Heaven and the old earth seemed to shrivel away, and I knew what love might mean, and God-like desire, and God-like surrender. I love you! All philosophy, all wisdom, religion, honour, manhood, hope, beauty lie in those words—I love you!" [1]

You can, also, burlesque plays and "pot" them as Mr. Pelissier is so fond of doing at the Apollo. Here is a specimen :—

THE POTTED "PAIR OF SPECTACLES."

Of the eleven characters in the piece, there are only two of any importance—the brothers Goldfinch. The only thing necessary to preserve is their personalities—carefully potted !

Don't be alarmed, this potted "pair" only plays about one minute.

Gregory. What are you selling for ? Do you think they'll drop ?

Goldfinch. No, but I want the money.

Gregory. What, are you hard up ?

Goldfinch. No, but a friend of mine is.

Gregory. What friend ?

Goldfinch. Ssh ! I can't tell you.

Gregory. So you are going to lend this money to a friend.

Goldfinch. Yes, and some more as well.

Gregory. What interest is he giving you ?

[1] Justin McCarthy : *If I were King.*

Goldfinch. I tell you he's a friend. When his ship is signalled—he'll repay me.

Gregory. I know that ship. It never will be signalled. I suppose that ship is your security?

Goldfinch. I want no security. I tell you he's a friend.

Gregory. I know that friend. Who doesn't? That friend has ruined as many men as drink. If I'd listened to that friend, I shouldn't be worth two hundred thousand pounds, but I didn't listen to him. I buttoned up my pockets—and I said, " No I've heard that story—tell me something new."

Goldfinch. You said that to a friend?

Gregory. I said, " Are you my friend? " He said, " I am." I said, " Do you want money? " He said, " Yes." I said, " The man who wants my money is no friend of mine."

Goldfinch. Gregory ! You say you're worth two hundred thousand pounds, but you are wrong. You are worth nothing ! For you are nothing more nor less than——

Gregory. Than what ? Go on—go on.

Goldfinch. Than—my brother. Forgive me.

Gregory. Now he's crying !

Goldfinch. You've taught me to suspect everybody, my wife, my son, my butler, my coachman, my shoemaker.

Gregory. They are all alike and we've potted the lot !

Goldfinch. " In much wisdom, is much grief, and he that increaseth knowledge, increaseth sorrow."

Gregory. Here ! You've got my spectacles !

Goldfinch. So I have.

Gregory. Here are yours. They got mixed up in the stew-pot !

Goldfinch. My old spectacles ! Now I see clearly ! I trust every one !

Gregory. We've left out my drunken scene !

Goldfinch. And my sparrow scene to slow music.

Gregory. Well they don't appear in the original French. Like me they come from Sidney Grundy !

It is an effective change to sometimes present your " imitations " in the form of sketches. I have presented several in this way. In a " Special Matinée " I imagined various leading stars rehearsing together. In " Impressions of Hamlet " I " took off " all the Hamlets I had seen. In " How I did my Aunt " I told how, to please my aunt, I took her to see several leading actors and actresses, but unfortunately this led her to suppose I was in the habit of spending my time in riotous living, and she was, in consequence, offended. She struck me out of her will, and determined to leave all her money to the " Dumb Friends' League ! "

If you find yourself unable to imitate individuals, you can burlesque types. Here are a few specimens :

The Exponent of the Legitimate Drama.

I thank you for this greeting kind and gracious.
Behold your greatest actor in the rôle
Of King and hero of this great assembly.
Withdraw ambitious supers from the limelight
Whilst I soliloquise, at length—alone !
D. T. or not D. T.—bad indigestion !
Whether 'tis better for the stalls to suffer,
When they attend Shakespearian revivals,
Also Grand Opera—Melba's throat's congested.
Stalls and Tiaras love Ta-ra-ra-boom-de-ay !
Songs patriotic—pirated editions—
To lie—two deep—to keep—to sleep—
Perchance to dream—ah ! there's the rub.
Where's the Prompter ?—Across what ?—
Across the road ! The thirsty little beast !
I'll make him stand me a drink—Prompter—Prompter !
(Exit)

A Comic Opera.

The scene is outside a village inn. The Chorus are sitting on rustic benches drinking. The comedian is flirting with the barmaid and melodiously calling for a drink :—

He. Give me a drink !

She. You shall be served.

He. My thirst is great !

Chorus. His thirst is great !

He. I'll drink the health of all the pretty girls.

Men. The pretty girls !

She. See, here's your drink.

Chorus. He's got his drink !

She. Just right I think.

He. Don't wink !

Men.   Don't wink, you very naughty little churls !

He.   I'm a foolish buffoon—I'm in love with the
moon
Or perhaps the same thing, with the child of
the King !

All.   Sing us a song descriptive of her beauty,
A song, a song, it is your bounden duty.

He.   Rosy lips and golden hair
Eyes like stars that grace the sky.
Peerless, priceless lady fair—
All is peace when thou art nigh !

All.   Bravo, bravo, you'll carry off the prize.
Your wondrous skill they'll duly recognize.
Oh, pray continue—

He.   (*nervous*).
Your tender charms are half divine,
Your presence fills us with delight,
Had I the power to make you mine
I'd cherish you both day and night—

All.   Ha ! Ha ! Ha ! Ha ! how well you sing.
Your art must please the Princess and the
King !

He.   (*more nervous*).
Your hair is gold, your eyes are blue,
Your hair is gold as I have said.
Your ears—I quite forget the hue !
Your teeth are black—no white—your
nose is red !

All.   Ha ! Ha ! You'll carry off the prize.
Your genius all must freely recognize !

.

He. Your jeers are splendid, they are quite sub-
　　lime.
Your laughter is thrice sweet to jester's ears,
But when I try a joke to perpetrate
And *want* a laugh I always have to wait.
But now a splendid motive I have found,
A jester in a very love-sick plight,
Theme for a story, full of mirth and joy.
When every joke and tale has left you cold
And at my choicest jests you turn away
I'll sing of love—you'll lend a ready ear,
And at this tragedy won't shed a tear,
Your laughs will rise when all my hopes are
　　dead
A love-sick jester with a heart of lead !
I've a jest for each time, and each season
　　and clime,
In the court or the glade, for each mistress
　　or maid,
For a peasant or king, I've a songlet to sing,
In the sunshine or rain, I've a joke most in-
　　sane.
I have stories galore—you have heard some
　　before,—
And my dancing's sublime, but my verses
　　won't rhyme.
But you'll laugh till you shake, and your
　　sides will soon ache
As I mimic all mimes, whom I've seen
　　several times.

I'm a fool!
    (*Chorus*) He's a fool!
Since a small tiny lad
When the dunce of the school
I was awfully bad
All my comrades would say
Both at work, and at play,
He's a fool!
    (*Chorus*) He's a fool!
Quite a fool!

THE LIGHT COMEDIAN.

My wife must never know! No. What a terrible situation! Robert, my boy, I'm a humbug. I went to Town last week. I found myself in Leicester Square at eleven o'clock at night. Don't ask me how I got there. I'd been dining! I wasn't quite, but I was near it! A beautiful creature rushed up to me. She put her arms round my neck and said " Protect me! " I never was so disturbed in my life. I said " Excuse me, I've important business. I cannot stop. I'll see you at the Sessions." I rushed away—made for a ' Taxi ' and said : " Drive me half a dozen times round Leicester Square! " I should have been arrested only somebody paid the bill. You went there too! You! You paid it too? You? Two pounds !—Two—oh, hang it !—my wife !

MUSICAL COMEDY.

No modern musical comedy is complete without a Plantation Song, sung in the Limelight with an invisible chorus. A young lady comes on in summer costume. Her dress suggests that a railway rug might be handy !

> Write a simple little song
> Never mind what it's about
> As long as there's a chorus
> That all the boys can shout !
> Just hint about de lovely gals
> And down by O-hi-o !
> I'll sing it in the limelight ;
> That song is sure to go !

Hushee ! O ! Hushee ! hush ! my Baby coon !
Hushee ! O ! Hushee ! Mamma's coming soon !
De Darkies am singing ! hushee ! don't ye cry !
Don't ye hear the ole Banjo ! Hushee ! By-bye !

CHAPTER XI

L'Envoi

WE have seen that there are two schools of Mimicry—the good and the bad ! We have taken a cursory glance at some exponents of the art. Let us hope you have learnt to pay attention to little details, to first principles ; that you have realized the necessity of analysing, classifying, comparing, thinking by analogy, and cultivating the histrionic sense.

Now my task is over. I have honestly tried to write a practical treatise on a difficult subject. There is no royal road to success. Labour constantly, and keep a good heart. Be indifferent to censure or adulation. Ignore those people who would strive to damp your ardour. Lead a healthy life, and accept my very best wishes for your success.

SOME PRESS OPINIONS

SATURDAY REVIEW.

Mimicry is a thing that has always interested me ; as is parody to literature, so (at its best) is mimicry to acting—a subsidiary art, but still, authentically an art. The two things have this further point in common : each of them is, for the most part, a speciality of youth. Read any undergraduate journal and you will find that it is mainly composed of parody, unconscious and conscious. Only a very precocious undergraduate has original thoughts or feelings. His soul is still vacant, gaping for the contents of other souls. It is still malleable, and may be from moment to moment moulded to any shape. Maturity fills it from within and fixes it, and thenceforth its owner has no power of parody, and no desire of parody. That is the normal course. But sometimes a mature man retains this desire and this power. . . . The power of mimicry deserts the average man at the same time, and for the same reason, as the power of parody. Before he is twenty the average youth can catch, more or less recognizably, the tone of voice and the tone of mind of his friends. Later, his own mind acquires so distinct a tone, and he becomes so accustomed to the sound of his own voice, that his efforts of mimicry (if he makes any) are dire failures. Occasionally, however, a man retains the knack even in his prime, and even though he has a distinct individuality. In him, and in him alone, do we behold the complete mimic. For mimicry is a form of criticism, and a distinct individuality—a point of view—is as needful in the mimic as in the critic. Mimicry that is a mechanical reproduction of voice and gesture and facial play is a mere waste of time and trial of patience. Yet that is the kind of mimicry that is nearly always offered to us. A man comes upon the platform and reproduces verbatim some scene of a recent play exactly as it was enacted by this or that mimic. If he were a parrot the effect would be amusing ; for it is odd to hear a bird uttering human inflections. But he happens to be a man, and so we are merely bored. His method being an exactly faithful reproduction of his subject's, we have no inclination to laugh, and the only pleasure we might be expected to gain would be when the subject were one for which we had a profound admiration ; but even so we should be more irritated than pleased. We should be wanting the real thing. An exact reproduction of the real thing can never be a satisfactory substitute. And if the average mimic is not a satisfactory substitute, what, in reason's name, is he ?

" The proper function of the mimic is, of course, like that of the parodist in words, or of the caricaturist in line, to exaggerate the salient points of his subject, so that we can, while we laugh at the grotesque superficial effect, gain sharper insight into the subject's soul, or, more strictly, behold that soul as it appears to the performer himself.

" This function is well understood and performed by Mr. J. Arthur Bleackley, whose imitations I heard last Monday at the Queen's Gate Hall. True, he is, to a certain extent, still influenced by the phonographic convention. His first imitation was of a well-known scene in *A Pair of Spectacles* enacted by Mr. Hare and Mr. Groves. But as soon as that was over he took the proper tack, riotously exaggerating how his subjects would appear if they were called upon to do some quite incongruous thing, and thus showing up clearly to us their peculiarities in the performance of appropriate and familiar things. Even better, as giving yet more scope for his critical instinct, was Mr. Bleackley's imaginary rehearsal of an imaginary play, in which all the leading mimes were to take part. Mr. Bleackley prefaced his entertainment with an earnest assurance that there was no malice in it, and that he had the most profound admiration for all his subjects. Strange that people do not understand that for any one to laugh at what he loves is quite as natural and inevitable in him as to laugh at what he hates, and that the only things which never amuse him are the things to which he is indifferent."

Max Beerbohm.

Morning Post.

" An entertainment, organized by Mr. J. Arthur Bleackley, was given yesterday afternoon at the Queen's Gate Hall, South Kensington, in aid of the Great Ormond Street Hospital for Children. There was a good attendance, and the entertainment was very successful. Mr. Bleackley himself appeared in a sketch entitled *A Special Matinée*, in which his portrayal of the accents and mannerisms of some of our best-known actors and actresses afforded intense enjoyment to the audience. Mr. Tree and Mrs. Patrick Campbell in particular were sketched to the life."

Daily Chronicle.

" Mr. J. Arthur Bleackley has a wonderful command of facial expression and vocal intonation, and has already given several successful entertainments."

Lady's Pictorial.

" Queen's Gate Hall was filled to overflowing by a very fashionable and appreciative audience when Mr. J. A. Bleackley gave his humorous and musical matinée in aid of Great Ormond

Street Hospital for Children. The chief feature of the entertainment was Mr. Bleackley's own inimitable imitations of popular actors and actresses, as heard in ' Leading Stars at Rehearsal,' his imitations of vocalists, in the latter part of the programme, recalling Mr. Corney Grain's style, and that of other artists, to perfection, in a charming and refined manner."

STAGE.

Γ " In the course of the afternoon Mr. Bleackley gave a number of imitations of actors, actresses and vocalists, prefacing his performance with the remark that they were ' good-natured caricatures,' after the manner of those of Max Beerbohm in a sister art. Some of these generally good imitations, were included in a new sketch showing ' Leading Stars at Rehearsal,' entitled *A Special Matinée.* In this Mr. Tree is supposed to be conducting a rehearsal of a new piece to be performed at a special matinée, and among the popular players concerned are Sir Charles Wyndham, Mr. George Alexander, Mr. Arthur Roberts and Mrs. Patrick Campbell. Mr. Bleackley also ' took off' Sir Henry Irving reciting ' Three Blind Mice,' Mr. John Hare and Mr. Charles Groves as the brothers Goldfinch in *A Pair of Spectacles*, Miss Ellen Terry in ' The Quality of Mercy' speech, Mr. Wilson Barrett in *The Sign of the Cross*, and Mr. Lewis Waller in *Monsieur Beaucaire*."

MANCHESTER COURIER.

" Mr. Bleackley is an entertainer of great power ; and perhaps the most delightful features of the concert were his imitations of most of the famous actresses and actors of the day. Imitators, like poets, are born, and not made, and no one who has not a great natural talent for this particular form of humorous art can ever hope to practise it with success. Mr. Bleackley evidently has quite unusual powers of mimicry, and his skits on his various victims were clever, true to life, and always good tempered. He was particularly successful in a little sketch of his own called *A Special Matinée*, in which he supposed an aspiring, if not a talented dramatic author to have engaged the services of a number of theatrical stars for the production of a play of his own. The stars in question were Mr. Beerbohm Tree, Mr. George Alexander, Mr. Arthur Roberts, Sir Charles Wyndham and Mrs. Patrick Campbell ; and his imitations of these popular favourites were exceedingly well done. His imitations of Sir Henry Irving and Mr. Lewis Waller reciting ' Three Blind

Mice ' were no less excellent, while among other famous actors whom he parodied were Mr. John Hare, Mr. Charles Groves, Mr. Wilson Barrett, Miss Ellen Terry.''

PALL MALL GAZETTE.

" Mr. Arthur Bleackley gave some amusing imitations of various well-known actors.''

THE QUEEN.

" Mr. Arthur Bleackley was inimitable in his imitations.''

DAILY TELEGRAPH.

" Some imitations, or, to speak more correctly, burlesques, of popular actors were given by Mr. Arthur Bleackley ; his suggestions of Sir Henry Irving, Messrs. Beerbohm Tree, Martin Harvey and Lewis Waller being so diverting that he was induced to add to the series Mrs. Patrick Campbell.''

M. A. P.

" Society has lately been pausing in its bridge to give an ear to the marvellous voice mimicry of Mr. Arthur Bleackley, and society must have profited by the experiment, for of all the imitators of actors and actresses the professional world of make-believe has yet yielded, surely Mr. Bleackley is the most surprising. To hear him speak a ' scene ' between Mrs. Patrick Campbell, as Paula, and Mr. George Alexander, as Aubrey Tanqueray, is to feel that there is, indeed, a second Mrs. Tanqueray in the air. . . . Miss Mary Moore and Sir Charles Wyndham are two of his principal victims, and his Lewis Waller and his Ellen Terry are both astonishingly correct.''

THE TABLE.

" Mr. Arthur Bleackley brought vividly before us some of the great actors and actresses of the day. It speaks well for the good feeling shown that these ' take offs ' can be tolerated even to a sort of amiable squabbling between Mr. and Mrs. Tree at rehearsal.''

GIL BLAS.

" M. Arthur Bleackley a parodié pittoresquement des artistes connus dans des improvisations spirituelles.''

REFEREE.

" The company was provided by Mr. George Ashton, and included Mr. Arthur Bleackley in a clever sketch entitled *How I did my Aunt*. In this lively trifle Mr. Bleackley introduced his inimitable imitations of all our most popular actors, and was lavishly applauded."

* * * * *

" Mr. Bleackley's ' impressions ' of Mrs. Patrick Campbell, Miss Mary Moore and Mr. Lewis Waller were singularly true to nature—only more so, of course, as the occasion demanded."

CROYDON ADVERTISER.

" Mr. Arthur Bleackley created much amusement. In *How I did my Aunt* he gives impressions of visits to various theatres, and has the happy knack of being able to pick out the peculiarities of many well-known actors, which, accentuated, are full of humour. Thus the audience are able to laugh at impersonations of Sir Henry Irving, Sir Charles Wyndham, Mr. Lewis Waller, Mr. Martin Harvey (' Hamlet '), Mr. George Alexander, Mr. Tree, Mrs. Patrick Champell, etc."

CROYDON CHRONICLE.

" Mr. Arthur Bleackley is clever and popular."

CROYDON GUARDIAN.

" *How I did my Aunt* is a sketch resolving itself into a series of really clever imitations of our most popular actors and actresses."

CROYDON CITIZEN.

" *How I did my Aunt* is the title of the act in which Mr. Arthur Bleackley appears with great success. In it he told how, to please his aunt, he took her to see several leading actors and actresses, but, unfortunately for him, this led her to suppose that he was in the habit of spending his time in riotous living, and she was in consequence offended. In telling the story Mr. Bleackley mimics the several ' stars ' he took his aunt to see. His mimicry of Mr. George Alexander and Mrs. Patrick Campbell were his best efforts."

SUSSEX DAILY NEWS.

" A great favourite. . . . His clever little recitals were one of the chief features, and his mimicry of well-known actors in *Impressions of Hamlet* delighted the audience."

WEEKLY TIMES.

" A remarkably clever mimic. His imitations are, perhaps, the best yet seen and heard in London."

FREE LANCE.

" Mr. Arthur Bleackley in a neat sketch which gracefully introduced his imitations of all our most popular actors was greatly applauded."

THE SHOWMAN.

" Mr. Arthur Bleackley gives some clever impersonations of celebrated artistes."

BRIGHTON GAZETTE.

" A clever impersonator."

*　　*　　*　　*　　*

" Mr. Bleackley pleased the audience with his admirable sketch, *Impressions of Hamlet*, and a humorous recitation entitled ' The Lancet,' which evoked much laughter."

M. A. P.

" Unsurpassably truthful imitations."

WESTMINSTER GAZETTE.

" The programme was contributed to by a number of theatrical celebrities. . . . One of the marked successes of the afternoon were the very clever impersonations of Mr. Arthur Bleackley."

THE PELICAN.

" Mr. Arthur Bleackley gave some clever imitations of well-known actors."

MORNING ADVERTISER.

" Capital imitations of Mr. Beerbohm Tree, Mrs. Patrick Campbell, Mr. George Alexander, Mr. Lewis Waller, Sir Charles Wyndham and Miss Mary Moore."

THE GENTLEWOMAN.

" Mr. Arthur Bleackley gave some very clever impressions of well-known artistes."

East Anglian Daily Times.

" A delightful programme of a miscellaneous character was presented by Mr. Arthur Bleackley.   Mr. Bleackley began with the well-told tale from *Percy's Reliques*, of ' King John and the Abbot,' which was made especially interesting by the histrionic powers of the reciter.   A couple of songs followed, selected from the repertoire of the late Corney Grain.   Though they were rendered with skill, they were scarcely in style up to the high level of Mr. Bleackley's elocution, which was again heard with abundant pleasure in Longfellow's powerful poem ' King Robert of Sicily.'   In his impressions of well-known artistes, Mr. Bleackley was entirely successful, and provoked a good deal of amusement, while his musical sketch, *Harmony Hall*, afforded scope for some clever humour and musical ability."

The Standard.

" Clever impressions."

The Evening Standard.

" Clever and amusing."

The Daily Mail.

" Mr. Arthur Bleackley's imitations are always welcome and original."

The Era.

" In each impersonation he gave evidence of marvellous powers of mimicry, and the scene between Mr. Tree and Mr. Roberts was extremely amusing."

Brighton Standard.

" A wonderfully facile caricaturist of the characteristic mannerisms of practically all the theatrical celebrities of the day.   The abstracted empyricism of Mr. Beerbohm Tree he hit off to perfection, and his imitation of Sir Charles Wyndham . was striking and significant,   Mr. Bleackley also ventured to imitate Ellen Terry and Mrs. ' Pat ' Campbell—and yet, allowing for the inevitable difference in the natural timbre of the masculine voice, the results in each case were remarkably graphic."

INDEX

Butler & Tanner, The Selwood Printing Works, Frome, and London.

WS - #0059 - 210223 - C0 - 229/152/8 - PB - 9781313776479 - Gloss Lamination